Let your creativity flow...

ode
limerick haiku
rhyme
ball...

- Inspirations From Northern Ireland
Edited by Aimée Vanstone

 Young**Writers**

First published in Great Britain in 2005 by:
Young Writers
Remus House
Coltsfoot Drive
Peterborough
PE2 9JX
Telephone: 01733 890066
Website: www.youngwriters.co.uk

SB ISBN 1 84602 253 3

Foreword

Young Writers was established in 1991 and has been passionately devoted to the promotion of reading and writing in children and young adults ever since. The quest continues today. Young Writers remains as committed to the fostering of burgeoning poetic and literary talent as ever.

This year's Young Writers competition has proven as vibrant and dynamic as ever and we are delighted to present a showcase of the best poetry from across the UK. Each poem has been carefully selected from a wealth of *Playground Poets* entries before ultimately being published in this, our thirteenth primary school poetry series.

Once again, we have been supremely impressed by the overall high quality of the entries we have received. The imagination, energy and creativity which has gone into each young writer's entry made choosing the best poems a challenging and often difficult but ultimately hugely rewarding task - the general high standard of the work submitted amply vindicating this opportunity to bring their poetry to a larger appreciative audience.

We sincerely hope you are pleased with our final selection and that you will enjoy *Playground Poets - Inspirations From Northern Ireland* for many years to come.

Contents

Tara Malcolmson (11)	27
Shannan Jackson (11)	27
Lucy Vella (11)	28
Leanne Herron (11)	28
Stuart Cairns (11)	29
Cheridan Andrews (9)	29
Debbie Casey (11)	30
Ryan Gibbons	30
Dean Gordon (11)	31
Rebecca Wills (10)	31
Katie McGowan (9)	32
Joshua Watson (11)	32
Adam Bailey (11)	33
Laura McVeigh (10)	33
Ryan Shaw (11)	34
Jake Redpath (11)	34
Scott Lindsay (11)	35
Nathan Barnes (10)	35
James Fegan (8)	36

Carrickfergus Model Primary School, Carrickfergus

Katy Kilpatrick (11)	36
Corey Jay Mayne (11)	37
Andrew Harrison (10)	37
Glenn Reynolds (11)	38
Jason Molloy (10)	38
William Bamford (11)	39
Jacob Sharpe (11)	39
Lauren Jones (11)	40
Jessica Boal (11)	40
Katie Topping (11)	41
Dale Colvin (11)	41
Bradley Gault (11)	42
Aimee Rea (11)	42
Craig Fletcher (11)	43
Rachel Beattie (11)	43
Rebecca Love (11)	43
Henry Atkinson (11)	44
Scott Kerr (11)	44
Lynsey Turner (11)	44
David Campbell (11)	45

Chloe Smyth (11)	45
Alex Burnside (11)	46
Emma Clarke (11)	46
Peter Brown (11)	47
James Simmonds (11)	47
Kerry McIlroy (11)	48
Victoria Brier (11)	48
Aimee Ellis (11)	48
Rachel Barkley (11)	49
Alex Thompson	49
Nathan Lyons (11)	49
Aaron Ellis (11)	50
Jessica Lyness (11)	50
Ashton Corey (10)	51
Laura McCurry (11)	51

Cornagague Primary School, Magheraveely

Dale Crudden (9)	52
Joe Mulligan (8)	52
Liam Óg Strain (9)	53
Holly Jenkins (8)	54
Cliona Mulligan (8)	55
Daniel McNally (8)	56
Killian Donohoe (10)	57
Domhnall Boyle (9)	58
Ciara McKenna (8)	59
Lois McCoy (8)	60
Denis Higgins (9)	61

Dungannon Primary School, Dungannon

Jonathan Sloan (9)	61
Jordan Stinson (10)	62
Graham McKinstry (10)	62
Karen Cardwell (10)	63
Nathan Boyd	63
Rachel Mullan (8)	64
Jamye McClung	64
Zoe Bartley (10)	65
Stephen Carlisle (9)	65
Ruth Burns (8)	66
Vickie Webb (8)	66

Joana Neves (9)	66
Tianna McCormack (8)	67
Axel Steen (8)	67
Hannah Jeffers (8)	68
Andrew Millar (11)	68
David McFarlane (8)	69
Simon Bartley (11)	69
Janine Ferry (8)	70
Hannah Clarke (8)	70
Ben Nixon (8)	71
Abby Anderson (8)	71
Jamie Reid (8)	71
Rebecca Emerson (8)	72
Chlöe Burton (10)	72
Darren Gilmore (8)	72
Thomas Downing (7)	73
Amy Willis (8)	73
Jake Turkington (8)	74
Micah Lambe (11)	74
Heather Maguire (11)	75
Janette Trimble (11)	76
Leah Cuddy (10)	76
Allan McGuffin	76
Jessica Rea (11)	77
Aimee Truesdale (11)	77
Dwaine Bradley (11)	77

Holywood Primary School, Holywood

Emily Johnson (10)	78
Connor Roberts (10)	78
Jordan Watts (10)	79
Abigail Dornan (10)	79
Rachael Berry (10)	80
Rhianna Uprichard (10)	80
Rebecca McLean (10)	81
Shannon Rice (10)	82
Amy McNally (11)	82
Joshua Danby (10)	83
Rosie Davies (11)	83
Marc Price (10)	84
William Burrows (10)	84

Katie Watson (11)	85
Siân Walker (10)	85
Laura McDowell (10)	86
Laura Edgar (10)	86
Jessica Cuthbert (10)	87
Emily Watts (10)	88
Alana Catherwood (10)	88
Sarah Wigston (11)	89
Lucy Rehill (11)	89
Rebecca Allen (10)	90
Suzy Harkness (11)	90
Caitlyn Adair (11)	91
Ross Adair (11)	91
Rachael Presho (11)	92
Dean Kane (10)	92
Tom Blair (10)	93
Rose Kerr (10)	93
Sophie Pollock (10)	94
Sarah Frost (10)	94
Chloe Cann (10)	95
Alex Roberts (10)	95
Amy Buchanan (10)	96
Brett Watts (10)	96
Brooke Burnside (10)	97
Rebecca Ferris (10)	97
Michael Robson (10)	97

Knockbreda Primary School, Belfast

Ross Neill (9)	98
Shannon McIntyre (10)	98
Sarah O'Neill (9)	99
Jordan Latimer (9)	99
Joel Turkington (9)	100
Hannah Nelson (9)	100
Aimee Gorman (10)	101
Matthew Deane (10)	101
Erin Healey (10)	102
Christine Collins (10)	102
Niamh Weir (10)	103
Ellie Neill (9)	103
Michael Anderson (10)	104

Bethany McDowell (9)	122
Andrew Hutton (11)	123
Robbie Johnston (9)	123
Lori Brown (10)	123
Elizabeth Brown (10)	124
Reuben Dooris (10)	124
Lauren McCormick (10)	125
Chloe Wilson (10)	125
Laura Bonnes (10)	126

Linn Primary School, Larne

Rebecca Duff (11)	126
Carolyn Humphrys (10)	127
Stuart McKay, Christopher Braniff & Jordan Mitchell (11)	128
Rachel Marks (9)	128
Judith Cameron (9)	129
Jenna Mulholland (9)	129
Jack Eland (11)	130
Aaron Hall (11)	130
David Murray (11)	131
Luke McKee (11)	131
Jilly Duddy (11)	132
Adam McCauley (11)	132
Clare McKay (11)	133
Rebecca Henry (9)	133
Dean McMeechan (10)	134
Heather McKinty (11)	135
Matthew Smit (11)	136
Caroline Duff (10)	136
David Fitzsimons (10)	137
Robert McKinley (11)	138
Scott McClelland (11)	139
Kim Hamilton (11)	140

Lisnasharragh Primary School, Belfast

Ross Mawhinney (8)	140
Anna Millan (8)	141
Caleb McCullagh (8)	141
Joshua Jared Campbell (8)	142
Katelyn Hamilton (8)	142
Laura Rainey (8)	143

Portglenone Primary School, Portglenone

Rostrevor Convent of Mercy Primary School, Rostrevor

St Joseph's Primary School, Downpatrick

St Joseph's Primary School, Newcastle

St Laurence O'Tooles Primary School, Belleeks

St Mary's Primary School, Kircubbin

Esther Flynn (10)   175
Holly Thompson (10)   175
Chloe McGreevy (10)   175
Stephen Hiles (10)   176
Lauren Fox (10)   176
Linda Murray (10)   176
Sarah Quinn (11)   177
Tanya Hiles (11)   177
Cori Marie Smyth (11)   178
Lucy Miskimmin (11)   178
Bernadette Clancy (11)   179
Ciaran Hughes (10)   179
Rebecca Martin (11)   180
Nicole Gilmore (10)   180
Kerry Savage (10)   181

St Patrick's Primary School, Craigavon
Brónách McNally (9)   181
Megan O'Neill (9)   182
Nuala McMahon (9)   182
Maeve Mulholland (9)   183
Zoe McKinstry (9)   183
Niamh Haddock (9)   184

Star of the Sea Girls' Primary School, Belfast
Chloe McLeish (9)   184
Bernadette McMullan (8)   185
Terri-Marie Morris (8)   185
Courtney Jean Moore (8)   185
Niamh Mowbray (9)   186
Catherine Murray (8)   186
Ashley Murray (8)   186
Katie O'Halloran (8)   187
Chelsea O'Hanlon (8)   187
Casey O'Shaughnessy (7)   187
Orla Thompson (8)   188
Lauren Tumelty (8)   188
Carol Anne Flynn (8)   188
Chloe Wilson (8)   189
Nicole Stitt (8)   189
Megan Joss (8)   189

Alice Doonan (8)	190
Christine Armstrong (9)	190
Natalie Faulkner (9)	190
Beth Neill (9)	191
Jeannine Brady (9)	191
Shannon Bright (9)	192
Shona Campbell (9)	192
Tammy Lee Begley (9)	193
Megan Kennedy (9)	193
Alysha Foster (9)	194
Talona Devlin (9)	194
Shauneen Cusick (9)	194
Caoimhe Diamond (9)	195
Sarah Louise Harper (9)	195
Nicole Brown (8)	195

The Cope Primary School, Armagh

Emily Bell (9)	196
Sarah-Louise Halligan (10)	196
Laura Brown (10)	196
Dora Nesbitt (10)	197
Michael Hook (9)	197
Jade Coleman (10)	198

Toreagh Primary School, Larne

Gareth Paisley (8)	198
Marc Robinson (8)	198
Keeleigh Hamilton (8)	199
Stuart Andrews (8)	199
Josh Hunter (8)	199
Andrew Weatherup (9)	200
Kirbi Stewart (9)	200
Jonathon Barry (8)	200
Philip Buchanan (8)	201
Sophie McDonald (8)	201
Michael Wilson (9)	201
Joshua Clarke (9)	202
Conor Brines (9)	202
Hannah McBride (8)	202
Thomas Magee (9)	203
Edward Horner (9)	203

The Poems

Darkness

I was in bed
In bed and sweating
I didn't want to go to sleep
I knew what would happen
10pm
It would be like last time
I would have a dream
No, it wasn't a dream
It was a living nightmare
11pm
I mean it when I say a living nightmare
I appear in a room like a sphere of darkness
At least
I think it's a room
12pm
I hear the chime of the clock
The cuckoo bird echoes
It's telling me to go to sleep
But I don't want to
1am
I am asleep
I knew I shouldn't have, but it was not my choice
I've entered the same nightmare again
I am afraid.

Matthew Pinkerton (10)
Abbey Primary School, Newtownards

Goodbye

The day has come
I've waited so long
Now I wish it had never come.

Here I am facing the tall narrow gates
I make my way through
Laughter coming from P6 children
Happiness fills the crisp, summer air.

They don't feel anything
They get to stay and play
Suddenly the bells ring
A shock goes through me like a hundred knives
I line up for the last time
But it doesn't feel the same
Mr Corbett comes out with a smile
But I know he feels the same
He takes us to class
I know he's sad inside.

The day has gone so fast
I didn't even think of it
Then suddenly before I know
It's time to say my goodbyes
As I walk through the deserted playground
I can almost hear the teachers cry
Tears start to drip off my cheek
As I say my goodbye.

Megan Stirling (11)
Abbey Primary School, Newtownards

The End Of A Journey

Only one more day
Then my 7 fun-filled childhood years are over.
I feel happy, I think
The 10am bell rings
One by one we disappear in
Knowing we are nearing an end
The day passes
The sun shines
Yet I don't want to go.
I want this day to last a lifetime
It's time to go
A tear comes to my eyes
I want to hide and not be found
Like a lost ghost
I say my final farewells
The doors burst open
Everyone laughs and screams
Except me
I feel like sprinting out that gate and not returning
But my heart is feeling pain
Feeling sadness
It's burning its way through
Slowly, delicately
My feet start to move
Memories flash past
Like angels bringing good news
The end, but a new beginning.

Loren McIntyre (11)
Abbey Primary School, Newtownards

Spring

Spring glides in
Fresh golden daffodils swaying in the breeze
Lambs prancing
Chicks dancing
In time to the spring rhythm
The sun shines down
Each ray contains happiness
Not a cloud in sight
Beautiful butterflies flutter around
Birds sing
In the cool spring breeze
Tulips sway
Like colourful balls of fire
Bluebells blow around
Softly swaying
In the silent night air
Dragonflies swoop over murky ponds
The dark nights are getting lighter
Children play beneath bright night skies
Eager
Waiting for summer to approach . . .

Trudi Irvine (11)
Abbey Primary School, Newtownards

Summer Sun

Summer sun
The sky is clear
The warm air blows around
The sun shines its heat rays
Onto the grassy ground
The lambs and chicks and sheep
Prance and dance about the field
And the children laugh and scream and play
Who knows what about
The smell of smoke from the barbecue
Fills the crisp summer air.

The air grows colder
The laughter disappears
As the clouds start to come
The summer sun vanishes
Behind clouds as dark as the midnight sky
I feel a spot of rain, then another and another
The summer day has ended
I look around, it's getting dark
Time to go inside.

Lauren Bunting (10)
Abbey Primary School, Newtownards

The Seven Year Wait

My brilliant life has flown in
Seven of the best years of my life have passed and gone
As the last time I will hear that bright red bell
Reminds me of that exciting day of P1
All the children shouting till now wandering through the gates
Wishing today would never end. The bell rings
All the wee ones run, shout and scream like wild animals.

Mr Corbett our P7 teacher wanders out to bring us in for the last time
The room is cleared, we have our last party together
But still it makes no difference to the way I feel
Down, tearful and wanting to go back to nursery
To start it all over again, back to having playtime
To doing the 11+.

At the end of the P7 year, classmates start to cry
Wishing that they could stay with Mr Corbett
Wandering out of the aged green gates
I say to myself, 'Why do I have to leave? Well this is the end
Goodbye I will come back to visit everyone again.'
I stroll home to start the last summer before secondary school.

Kirsty Legge (11)
Abbey Primary School, Newtownards

The End Of Primary School

It's the last day
Everyone is playing outside
Everyone happy as it's the last day
As the bell rings
Everybody runs to get in line
I think
It's the last time I will hear it.
When we go in we have a lot of fun
Playing games and eating food
But everybody is feeling sad about leaving
When it is time to go home
Some people run out like wild animals
And others are still walking out with friends
Saying tearful goodbyes
As I go out
I am surrounded by my memories
They are mostly good
As I look back at the school
A tear comes to my eye.

Jane Patton (11)
Abbey Primary School, Newtownards

Bye-Bye Primary School

The last day has finally arrived
P6's shout and scream with joy
Wandering through the crowded playground
I think of all the exciting games we invented and played
The bell rings
We are greeted by a smiling Mr Corbett
As we are led into the classroom
We sit down at our usual seats and wait
Wait to go to our very last assembly
In the last assembly we sing the last hymns
Leaving at a quarter past twelve the emotions unravel
I cry as I say my last goodbyes
Slowly walking through the half-empty playground
I remember all the laughing the playground was filled with
                                        at break time and lunchtime
My emotions overtake me
The end of one chapter
The start of another.

Rebecca McDowell (11)
Abbey Primary School, Newtownards

A Boy Called Jake

There once was a young boy called Jake
Who once did have a pet snake
He got in a fit
When he fell in a pit
And the snake had eaten his cake.

Jake Brown (11)
Abbey Primary School, Newtownards

Young Writers - Playground Poets - Inspirations From Northern Ireland

The Times I Shouldn't Forget

Seven years have been and gone
I wish this day would never come
Wandering through the deserted playground
I come to a halt
All my memories surround me
Some good, some bad
But the ones that won't go away are
The ones of the good times
Some of the ones with my friends on a school trip
And some of the jokey teachers
I must never forget
Now I keep on walking through the school gate
I look back and remember
The times I've been running round
Like an animal from a pack
Tears start dripping from my eyes to my cheek
I must never forget the time I've had.

Kirsty Turner (11)
Abbey Primary School, Newtownards

The Lonely Nights

As the misty clouds sweep over the pale white orb that is the moon
The night grows darker, full of mystery, full of wonder.
The dark shadows of the forest, unmoving, silent sinister
They surround the cool, black air,
Like frozen phantoms from a fantasy world.

The lonely wolf howls, longing for his lost family,
The cold breeze brushing against his grey fur
The want in his heart, the need in his heart
For the relatives he has never known.

As the sun begins to rise
The black night is replaced by an amber dawn,
As the birds begin to sing their happy morning song,
The lonely night has disappeared, though it shall come again.

Megan Higgins (11)
Abbey Primary School, Newtownards

Ending

Tick-tock, tick-tock,
the end is here
the clock has stopped
as the last day vanishes
in thin air
can't it wait?
It isn't fair
as I wave goodbye.

Seven years
it passed like light
as the end nears
causing a narrow gap
of primary learning
for they don't understand
that everything I was earning
is behind me now.

The bell vibrates
ringing throughout
the school and gates
the misty memories clog my mind
see you friends
I will miss you
I'm sorry it ends
I'm sorry, I'm sorry.

Karl Halliday (11)
Abbey Primary School, Newtownards

The Final Day

I did not want this day to come
I have waited for six years now
And I hate this day.

Lonely I go to the door
Through the empty playground
No one saying, 'Yeha, ha, no school.'

The sun shines on the school
It's OK for them
They go into classes next year.

My loud, sweet bell rings
Going into my mind one more time
Slowly I walk into the school.

The morning is not right for me
Mr Corbett takes us up
I think he is upset too.

The day evaporates
Like it was a daydream
I now am saying my goodbyes.

I am second to go
As I am running fast to catch my chap
Through the lonely footpath.

iuuuuuuuuu+I could just hear some people
Saying, 'Don't forget us.'
I shouted back, 'I will never forget, *never.'*

Ross Stannage (11)
Abbey Primary School, Newtownards

Winter

Winter creeps in
Jack Frost is near
The first is special
Others follow the leader
A cup of powdery snow
Before you know
A blanket of dreams
Bare trees decorated
With sparkling angels
The red fiery-breasted creature
Is sent from above
As the fox runs like
A mysterious shadow
A frozen liquid in the midnight sky
Reflected in a clear, crystal, frozen pond
A howl runs free
The strike of fear
The crash of spite
A sudden ray of happiness
The colours of winter have vanished
The fantasy colours will live!

Nicola Irvine (10)
Abbey Primary School, Newtownards

It's All Gone Tomorrow

I've treasured this day
From P1 up
But now that it's here
I can't stand it
The shouts and laughter
Bring tears to my eyes
All right, school's over
For a while
Not for me
I won't be back next year.
My dream of someday leaving
Seems more like a nightmare now.
They don't know what it's like
When this day finally comes.
The tears gush out
Like a running river stream
While I say my goodbyes
My heart beats wild
And there's a lump in my throat
I say goodbye to my teachers
From P1 to P7
I say to each one
I promise I will never forget you.

Benjamin Gribben (11)
Abbey Primary School, Newtownards

It Won't Happen Again

I wake up and get ready
I don't think of this day
As being the last day
I arrive at the gates
But they look different
Everything looks different
We began to play football
But I don't play my best
Bell rings
We line up
Mr Corbett arrives
To take us to the classroom
For the last time
We have our party
Everyone seems happy
But I don't think they are
Bell goes
We all leave
We say our goodbyes
As I walk out the gate
I turn round for one last look
It was as if the gates closed
And locked themselves
They're saying,
'You'll never be back.'

Andrew Armstrong (11)
Abbey Primary School, Newtownards

Tears Start As The Day Dawns

Seven years gone already,
Doesn't feel like it
Sad Mr McDade says hello to kids
Bell rings and the children run to their lines.

Teachers come out with happy faces,
But we know they're sad,
They bring us to our classrooms
And the eyes start to water.

You can hear the P6's jumping about
They're OK - they come back next year,
I can't believe this day has come,
How can I say goodbye to all my friends?

I want to cry, but my eyes won't let me,
Children have made swimming pools already
Mr Corbett opens his presents as a tear falls down his cheek,
The day goes fast as we say farewells.

We say goodbye to our past teachers,
Then to Mr Corbett,
We line up to go home,
Walking down the stairs, sadness hangs in the air.

In the playground we hug our friends goodbye,
'See you soon, give me a call.'
We wander up the path like wanderers in a desert,
Goodbye Abbey, see you soon.

Rachel Kelly (12)
Abbey Primary School, Newtownards

End Of An Era

Day after day
They pass quickly
Too fast to stop.

And it's the last day
For me in Abbey Primary
The end of my saga.

A near decade in this school
I've had
And it ends today.

People may cheer when the clock strikes twelve
On this vibrant day
But not me however, not me.

The playground is deserted
It all ends here
I'm not a pupil of this school anymore.

The bell has gone
But can't it wait
Can't it wait?

The playground is barren
Like the vast Gobi desert
As I salute the sky.

It is all but over
The year is gone
It's the end of an era.

Karl Poots (11)
Abbey Primary School, Newtownards

Last Day

I'm walking through the school gates ready to play football
one last time

I wish it hadn't come to this
Some people happy, some sad, some angry, some mad.
I have a sick feeling in my stomach
Seven years I've waited, seven years I've clung on
It's time to move on now, I'll be first year next
I hear everyone else shouting and screaming
It's all right for them, they can come back, but I can't.
I feel like overflowing my emotions
Bell rings
I see Mr Corbett standing there
We go to class, have a party
But me, I don't feel like partying
Not today.
I look back on all my memories
The day, like a spirit, fades away
I'm going to my old teachers and saying goodbye
And before I know it I'm crying.
I don't want to leave
School's like home
I'm walking the boulevard of broken dreams
Through the ghostly playground my eyes are ready to burst
like water taps

It's my turn to walk the lonely road
I take one last look
People shouting out saying look after yourself
I walk away sadly, the end has finally come.

Gareth McGimpsey (11)
Abbey Primary School, Newtownards

Lost Memories

Here I am facing the tall grand gates
I've waited a long time for this day to finally come
I put one foot in front of the other
And before I know it I'm standing inside the school gates
My heart is racing and my knees are shaking
All around me I hear laughter and cheers of joy
They don't have a clue how I feel
They're going to be here next year
I'm not
The bell rings and soon it hits me inside
I try to memorise the ringing of the bell
Over and over again inside my head
For I will never hear it again
We line up as Mr Corbett walks out
Everyone is silent
Like a deserted sandy island on a warm summer's day
The day vanishes into the misty air
In the distance far away
I say my farewells as a tear trickles down my rosy cheek
As I wander through the deserted playground
I can hear the ringing of the morning bell
Running through my head over and over again
There it will stay forever.

Sacha Curry (11)
Abbey Primary School, Newtownards

Eagle's Eyes

(Eagle's Eyes is a poem about a girl who is afraid of the dark)

The moon watches over me
With eagle's eyes
As the clouds dance
In midnight blue
The glittering stars watch
But yet the lonely moon
Watches over me
With eagle's eyes
Shooting stars fly across
The sparkling sky
But the moon still watches over me
With eagle's eyes
I fall asleep
As the moon whispers softly
I will always watch over you
With soft eagle's eyes
I promise.

Hannah McAlees (11)
Abbey Primary School, Newtownards

Litter

People throwing litter on the ground,
Turning our environment round and round.
Polluting our environment isn't nice,
Even if you only do it once or twice.
Reduce the litter,
Or the Earth will be bitter.
Reduce, reuse, recycle,
Wake up to waste!

Rameen Loughlin (10)
Abercorn Primary School, Banbridge

Environment

Every day, landfill sites fill and grow like mountains,
Now we must kill the landfill and pollution.
Very messy is the street, dying animals that we meet.
In the houses, vandalism is not what we seek.
Reduce, reuse, recycle is what we should be doing.
Across the country the councils are trying hard with their initiatives.
If we recycle, the world will be a better place,
Men and women seem happy enough - but are they?
Environmental health is increasingly worrying,
No one can afford not to take action to save our world.
Try to recycle for the sake of mankind's future!

Stuart English (10)
Abercorn Primary School, Banbridge

Spring Days

The months of spring are March, April and May,
All the children come out and play.
It starts to get light,
Good weather to fly a kite.

The flowers start to bloom,
It is nearly June.
In spring it is nice to walk,
You could bring a mate and talk.

It's time to go to bed,
Time to rest your weary head.
Time to say good day,
It's spring, hip hip hooray!

Hannah Gribbin (10)
Abercorn Primary School, Banbridge

It's Your Rubbish, Sort It Out!

I like Sprite,
But I don't like the bottles on the ground.

I like Coke in a can,
But I don't like the can on the ground.

Why not recycle?

I like crisps,
But I don't like their packets on the ground.

I like sweets,
But I don't like the wrappers on the ground.

Why not put them in the bin?

I like to go out and shop down the town,
But it isn't a pretty sight,
To see all the rubbish on the ground.

So sort it out!

Laura McKee (10)
Abercorn Primary School, Banbridge

Pollution

P ut the rubbish in the bin,
O zone layer is getting thin,
L eave something for the next generation,
L ose the smoke, keep it clean,
U ntimely deaths we can avoid.
T ry and recycle,
I llness and disease will kill,
O bserve the Earth, be friendly to it
N ow let's stop pollution for the environment!

Matthew Connolly (10)
Abercorn Primary School, Banbridge

My Brilliant Spell

I'm in the mood to cast a spell
And I'll do it really well!

Tongue of cow, any how,
Spider's web, bird's bed,
Rat's fur, pussy cat's purr,
Rabbit's ears, children's fears,
Swan's wings, person's rings,
Pig's eyes, big black flies,
I think will do the spell.

The scales of a shark, a seal's bark
Blind wasp's sting, makes a ting,
Monkey's bum, human's thumb,
An elephant's trunk, a baboon's bunk,
A giraffe's neck and a bird's peck.

This is my spell completely done
Let's go out and have some fun!

Hayley Robb (11)
Abercorn Primary School, Banbridge

Egypt

In Egypt the pyramids stand so tall
The weather is so dry
They stand higher than the garden wall
The weather is so hot it makes me want to cry.

The weather is so hot
The pyramids are so gold
The stars are twinkling a lot
At night the weather is so cold.

Jennifer Loughlin (9)
Abercorn Primary School, Banbridge

My Spell

This is a spell,
A very powerful spell,
Take cover if you dare.
Toad's slime,.
Cat's eyes
And of course, some human hair.
Bat's wings,
Other things,
Watch out!
It's bubbling now.
A wolf's ear,
A drop of fear.
We're almost done,
This is going to be fun!
Boom!
An echo fills the room,
I'm standing in rubble,
But there is one thing I can do
And that is, cause *trouble!*

Sarah Moffett (11)
Abercorn Primary School, Banbridge

My Best Friend

My best friend is yellow.
he is a summer in Australia.
Like a red-hot furnace.
He is a flash of lightning
And a pair of jeans and a shirt.
He is like an old rocking chair
And is the same as Tom and Jerry.
He is a plate of concrete chips.

Adam Hoey (11)
Abercorn Primary School, Banbridge

Springtime Is Here!

The lambs are born,
So soft and white,
The farmers start to plough the corn
And spring is such a beautiful sight.

The little chicks are so soft and fluffy
The sound they make goes cheep, cheep, cheep.
They look so fat and puffy,
While the lambs jump and leap.

The foals go trotting by their mum,
Jumping and skipping all day long,
The birds in the trees let out a little hum
And spring is almost gone.

Kari-Anne Proctor (8)
Abercorn Primary School, Banbridge

Spring Days

April weather day
Sunny, clear or showers,
All the children play
Sun shining on our cars.

The clothes are lighter,
Bandannas, hats and tops
The nights are brighter
It's time to eat lollipops.

We have a barbecue
To finish off the night
It is just for me and you
It is such a lovely sight.

Lara Kerr (9)
Abercorn Primary School, Banbridge

Spring Is Here

Spring is here, winter's gone,
Now it's time to have some fun
Birds are starting to sing their song,
Lambs like to skip and run.

Chicks are hatching from their eggs,
Buds are appearing on the trees,
Chicks with tiny little legs,
We start to see bees.

We can have lots of fun,
It puts me in a good mood,
In May we get more sun,
Spring is good.

Sarah Dillon (9)
Abercorn Primary School, Banbridge

Creepy Crocs

If you want to meet a crocodile,
You really should think twice,
Because if you run into one,
It surely won't be nice,
First they'll drag you underwater,
Down, down, until you drown.
They'll eat you up all in one go,
Then down the river you will flow,
In the stomach of the beast
Meanwhile, the crock has enjoyed its feast.
Crocs are such ferocious creatures
And they have some amazing features.
Crocs are strong and very hostile
Maybe now you'll stay away for awhile!

Carrie Honeyford (11)
Abercorn Primary School, Banbridge

Crocodile Rap

Down in the river,
He'll eat your liver,
If he smells your arm,
That's his food alarm!

You better be alerted,
When he's asserted,
We are his dishes,
Because he is vicious.

He is mightier,
Than a street fighter,
He is outstanding,
When he's demanding.

The croc will get his relation,
During the wildebeest migration,
Buy his scales in a shop,
That's the end of the crocodile rap.

Ryan McBurney (11)
Abercorn Primary School, Banbridge

The Crocodile

He waits around for his annual feast
People say he is a magnificent beast.
He looks for food and smells for blood
He swims in water and lurks in the mud.
He looks around with his great big eyes
And kick starts with his muscular thighs.
He's just as dangerous as a great white shark.
He hunts in the light and sleeps in the dark.

Arthur Kelly (11)
Abercorn Primary School, Banbridge

Crocodile Crew

When you see
A crocodile sunning,
Don't go near
Or you'll end up running!

When you think
A croc is sleeping,
Don't go near
You'll end up weeping!

If it sees
A lovely sight,
Be careful, it
Might take a bite!

If crocs eat a
Human or a deer
That will probably last
Him for another year.

Tara Malcolmson (11)
Abercorn Primary School, Banbridge

Crocodiles

C is for carnivorous, he will eat you up.
R is for ravenous, the ever hungry crocodile.
O is for obnoxious, what a horrid thing he is.
C is for cunning, as he hides from his prey.
O is for obdurate, a hard-hearted stubborn creature.
D is for dangerous, keep well away!
I is for independent, of what a crocodile is.
L is for lazy, sleeping all the time.
E is for energetic, when he catches his prey.
S is for scaly and very, very scary!

Shannan Jackson (11)
Abercorn Primary School, Banbridge

Crocodile

Tail swerving here and there,
Welcome to the crocodile's lair,
His large teeth and bulging eyes,
Make up a face you will despise.

Mysteriously lurking in the bog,
He looks like a floating log,
But when his eyes come into view,
You will know he's after you.

Agile body, mighty jaw,
He will eat his victims raw,
Animals that look at him,
Will all fear his fearsome grin.

But sometimes I think he's sad,
That is why he's acting bad,
Something makes him lonely,
I hate to see him in despair.

Lucy Vella (11)
Abercorn Primary School, Banbridge

A Big Crocodile

A big crocodile
Is slimy and green
A big crocodile
Has a cheesy grin
A big crocodile
Could swallow you in one bite
A big crocodile could sleep all night
A big crocodile could eat a deer
But that would last him for a whole year.

Leanne Herron (11)
Abercorn Primary School, Banbridge

Werewolf Spells

Now it's time to chant our spell
And this is one we will not tell

The eye of an ogre, the ear of a crook
A grown man's shoulder, an elephant's foot.
Stir it well around and around
Make sure that it doesn't touch the ground.

Mrs Semple spins around with Orlando Bloom
We stir the potion with a golden spoon.

A werewolf's hair and a claw of a bear.
A sheet of fur from a fully grown hare.
Then shed the crocodile's scaly skin
And take its teeth from that silly grin.

Mrs Semple spins around with Orlando Bloom
We stir the potion with a golden spoon.

A wing of a bat, the tail of a rat
The insides of a few blind mice.

Mrs Semple spins around with Orlando Bloom
We stir the potion with a golden spoon.

Now it's time to test our spell
All I hope is that everything goes well.

Stuart Cairns (11)
Abercorn Primary School, Banbridge

Recycle

R educe, reuse, recycle,
E nvironment is being destroyed,
C aring people realise our environmental sin,
Y ou must keep the streets clean,
C lear the rubbish off the roads,
L et's stop throwing down litter, put it in the bin,
E verything is clean now, we can have a better life now.

Cheridan Andrews (9)
Abercorn Primary School, Banbridge

Snap, Snap

Snap snap, crunch crunch,
I shall have an early lunch!

Oops there goes a leg,
Now you have to use a peg,
I am very vicious,
I need a great variety of dishes,
I will bite off your arm,
It will do you great harm,
I think I shall bite a head,
Then I shall go to bed.

Snap snap, crunch crunch,
I shall have an early lunch!

Debbie Casey (11)
Abercorn Primary School, Banbridge

Killer Crocodile

Beware of him as he likes blood
He lurks in water or in the mud
He's known to be a vicious beast
Kills a buffalo for his feast.

He lazes around every day
He doesn't have to do what you say
He will eat everything in sight
He isn't really very polite.

If you touch him it's the end of you
And maybe even an animal or two
You'll find him in the Amazon or the Nile
Beware he is a crocodile!

Ryan Gibbons
Abercorn Primary School, Banbridge

A Wonderful Charm

Listen, listen I want a nibble
This is not a silly scribble.

A fox's bed and its head
Hairy monkey's arm
Oh! What a wonderful charm!
Every rat's eye
That's no lie.
From a cat I'll get a hair
Even though it might stare.
A nose of a doe
Now this will flow
This is going to be some show!

I could make a twin
But I just have to add a pin
And if anyone drinks
They will laugh in kinks.

Dean Gordon (11)
Abercorn Primary School, Banbridge

The Crocodile Crew

I say you'd have to be sly to fight this guy
You'd have to be cunning or you'll end up running
Because someone like you will never beat him or his crew
We need someone fast who will run right past
We need someone brave for they'll get a brutal beating
Oh boy he's a gigantic freak!
He won't be messed with so don't be teasing
He's horrifying it's daunting that's true
He wants you!
Fighting a croc you'll get a shock
So never try to fight a croc!

Rebecca Wills (10)
Abercorn Primary School, Banbridge

Autumn

In the autumn days when nights grow longer,
The farmers are harvesting the corn,
Children like having conker fights,
But the days are not very warm.

Birds migrate for winter,
Hedgehogs hide under leaves,
Squirrels collect nuts for their store
And the trees wave about in the breeze.

Hallowe'en is coming soon,
We dress up as goblins and ghouls
And go out trick and treating,
Looking like little fools.

In the autumn wind the leaves are falling,
Falling to the ground,
Twisting, turning, whistling, whirling,
Barely making a sound.

The leaves are changing colour
To yellow, brown and red,
We think of all these autumn things,
As we lie upon our beds.

Katie McGowan (9)
Abercorn Primary School, Banbridge

A Crocodile

It's a terrifying creature
With eyes as big as apples,
Teeth as long as daggers,
Feet as large as tables.
It shows no mercy
It can be lazy or fast
It is hardly ever hungry.
It lives in a swamp
It is green all over
It's a crocodile!

Joshua Watson (11)
Abercorn Primary School, Banbridge

Spin And Bubble Lots of Trouble

A cat's guts and shark's fin
Slimy eels and a fish skin
Monkey's tail and bat's wings
Sea horse's head and polar bear's claw
An ogre's toe and mermaid's tail
Newt's eye and little boy's thigh
Flamingo's beak and plenty of cheek
Penguin's feet and parrot's colourful tail
Rhino's horn, the monster's born
If you want to bring trouble come and
Drink my trouble bubble.

Adam Bailey (11)
Abercorn Primary School, Banbridge

Witch's Spell

(Based on 'Macbeth')

Double, double toil and trouble,
Fire burn and cauldron bubble.

Eye of snake, wing of bat,
Beak of bird, tooth of shark,
Some bacon fat and the tail of a cat,
The ear of a pig and a nice fresh fig,
A cat's whiskers and a few blisters,
The head of a dog and the tongue of a frog.

You had better be on the lookout,
For you're in trouble without a doubt.

Laura McVeigh (10)
Abercorn Primary School, Banbridge

My Spell

Watch out watch out,
Without a doubt,
The potion I make
Will make you shake.

Guts of dog, brain of frog,
Eye of troll, leg of foal,
Tail of snake, blood of human,
Heart of demon,
Livers of shark, slime from bark.

My spell is finished, you'd better run,
For in a second you will shake
And all your organs will disintegrate!

Ryan Shaw (11)
Abercorn Primary School, Banbridge

My Horrible Spell!

This spell will help me to grow wings
And fly away to Alice Springs.

Bat's wing, wasp's sting,
Tip of nail, snake's scale,
Cat's tail, hope this spell doesn't fail.

Snail's slime, yes, it's fine,
Horse's hoof, burnt-down roof,
Sheep's liver, it makes you shiver.

The ingredients for this fabulous spell,
Are not anywhere that I can tell.

Jake Redpath (11)
Abercorn Primary School, Banbridge

To Make You Go Pink

In this pot if you drink
It will turn you fluorescent pink.

Tail of monkey, leg of donkey
Wing of fly, ogre's eye
Wing of bat, tail of rat
Tongue of dog, foot of hog
Tail of seal, orange peel
Eye of frog, bark of dog
Human brain and some fine grain
Teacher's eye and a big black fly!

All this, put into the pot
It makes up a perfect plot.

Scott Lindsay (11)
Abercorn Primary School, Banbridge

Pollution

P rotect our future!
O ur air is filthy,
L ove our Earth.
L itter lies everywhere,
U se your recycling bin,
T ry to be energy efficient.
I llness and disease can be prevented,
O ur precious world is in danger
N ever throw litter down!

Nathan Barnes (10)
Abercorn Primary School, Banbridge

n place,
d the River Nile,
keep up your pace,
for miles and miles.

lace to be happy,
Y   just hear the mummies groaning,
So don't stop to change the baby's nappy,
Or you could be the next one moaning!

James Fegan (8)
Abercorn Primary School, Banbridge

Groups

A munch of apples
A chitter of girls
A cauldron of witches
A giggle of clowns

A crunch of crisps
A run of rabbits
A screech of violins
A sweetness of sweets

A think of drinks
A pitch of boys
A noise of pupils
A print of computers

A glow of lights
A shimmer of glitter
A smell of flowers
A fluff of cats.

Katy Kilpatrick (11)
Carrickfergus Model Primary School, Carrickfergus

The Writer Of This Poem

(Based on 'The Writer of this Poem' by Roger McGough)

The writer of this poem
Is as sparky as a firework
As keen as the clockwork
As cool as ice . . .

As strong as an ox
As sharp as a knife
As dark as a winter's night
As tough as diamond . . .

As bold as a lion
As skilful as a boxing glove
As ferocious as a fire
As handsome as a prince

The writer of this poem
Is the best in the universe
He's as cool as ice
(Or so I say and think!)

Corey Jay Mayne (11)
Carrickfergus Model Primary School, Carrickfergus

Loudly

Loudly the bells rang,
Loudly the children sang.
Loudly the stereo played,
Loudly the engine rummed.

Loudly the motorbike drove,
Loudly stomping in Finchley Grove.
Loudly as a classroom,
Loudly the people shouted in the brass room.

Andrew Harrison (10)
Carrickfergus Model Primary School, Carrickfergus

The Writer Of This Poem

(Based on 'The Writer of this Poem' by Roger McGough)

The writer of this poem
Is smaller than a tree
As fast as the wind
As smooth as the current

Is strong as steel
As good as me
As smart as a tick
As clear as a ghost

Is as funny as a clown
As bright as the sun
As brave as a shark
As clean as a whistle

The writer of this poem
Never ceases to amaze.

Glenn Reynolds (11)
Carrickfergus Model Primary School, Carrickfergus

Loudly

Loudly is a sports car racing down the road,
Loudly is a bomb ready to explode,
Loudly is teacher yelling all she has,
Loudly is a bulldozer knocking down some flats.

Loudly is a gun that has just been shot,
Loudly is a plane ready to take off,
Loudly is a waterfall landing on the ground,
Loudly is a drum making such a sound.

Jason Molloy (10)
Carrickfergus Model Primary School, Carrickfergus

A Splash Of Sprite

A cauldron of witches
The tails of cats
Eye patches of pirates
A circus of clowns

Roars of lions
Fields of oxen
A party of people
A database of computers

A lasso of cowboys
A planet of spacemen
A scream of girls
A ring of boxers

A case of pencils
A car of wheels
A book of pages
And nice tasty meals.

William Bamford (11)
Carrickfergus Model Primary School, Carrickfergus

Loudly!

Loudly the baby cries for attention
Loudly the car's brakes screeching
Loudly the gun bangs and flashes
Loudly the glass smashes

Loudly the teacher shouts
Loudly the cupboard door bangs
Loudly the old man snores
Loudly bombs the earthquake
Loudly the bell rings.

Jacob Sharpe (11)
Carrickfergus Model Primary School, Carrickfergus

A Bark Of Dogs

A wrinkle of a Shar-Pei
A purr of cats
A wiggle of worms

A bounce of rabbits
A growl of wolves
A spot of Dalmatian

A horn of rhinoceros
A cheep of birds
A crackle of rubbish

A jump of horses
A fly of butterflies
A bark of dogs.

Lauren Jones (11)
Carrickfergus Model Primary School, Carrickfergus

A Mosaic Of Tiles

A hose of water,
A grudge of complaints,
A fashion of daughters,
A calendar of dates,
A game of goners,
A shower of mates,
A folder of files,
A head full of lies,
A mosaic of tiles.

Jessica Boal (11)
Carrickfergus Model Primary School, Carrickfergus

The Writer Of This Poem

(Based on 'The Writer of this Poem' by Roger McGough)

The writer of this poem,
Is as cool as ice,
As cuddly as a bear,
But with a bit of spice.

As soft as a rabbit,
As crazy as two-year-olds,
With spending money as a habit
And wish to have a million golds.

As quick as a mouse,
As tidy as my brother,
As tall as a toy house,
As different as my mother.

The writer of this poem
Loves to be surprised
And has hazel eyes.

Katie Topping (11)
Carrickfergus Model Primary School, Carrickfergus

The Writer

(Inspired by 'The Writer of this Poem' by Roger McGough)

The writer is like a bull
As strong as an ox
As fast as a cheetah

As good as Liverpool
As sweet as a sweetie
As sharp as a sword
As wild as a beast
As loud as a lion
As bouncy as a trampoline.

Dale Colvin (11)
Carrickfergus Model Primary School, Carrickfergus

Adverb Poem

Gently the feather fell on the grass
Brightly the sun shone on the ground
Swiftly the frog jumped off the leaf into water
Loudly the elephant trotted out of the zoo
Lightly the bee landed on the flower
Loudly the boy jumped on his mother's bed
Swiftly the robbers stole the diamonds
Brightly the torch glowed into the dark
Gently the raindrop hit the water
Loudly the train horn went off.

Bradley Gault (11)
Carrickfergus Model Primary School, Carrickfergus

What Is The Moon?

A moon is a white golf ball,
In a black bag,

The moon is like a circle light,
In a dark room,

The moon is like a clock,
Being fixed on a dark table,

The moon is a circular white rubber,
In a brown dark pencil case,

The moon is a blank piece of paper,
Put onto a blank piece of card.

Aimee Rea (11)
Carrickfergus Model Primary School, Carrickfergus

Softly

Softly is like a feather dropping on the ground
Softly is like a baby sleeping
Softly is like a bit of cotton
Softly is like a bird gliding through the sky
Softly is like stroking a cat
Softly is like a kiss
Softly is like a baby's bum
Softly is like writing on a page.

Craig Fletcher (11)
Carrickfergus Model Primary School, Carrickfergus

Sea

The sea gives out a lashing roar
It bobbles up and down
It eats away at the edge of the cliffs
And gives a gigantic frown.
Suddenly it goes all calm
And rolls around on its belly
He changes its feelings
And eats a bowl of jelly.

Rachel Beattie (11)
Carrickfergus Model Primary School, Carrickfergus

Softly

Softly is a baby's first time walking,
Softly is a feather falling.
Softly is the way you brush your hair,
Softly is the way your stroke something so rare.

Softly is the way you kiss in love,
Softly is the flutter of a dove.
Softly is a child blinking,
Softly is a person thinking.

Rebecca Love (11)
Carrickfergus Model Primary School, Carrickfergus

No!

No is a black word,
It is as dark as death,
As fateful as falls,
As greeting as graves,
As ripe as rhubarb,
it is as deathly as the Devil,
No is a nocturnal night,
As candleless as caves,
It is as cool as cool,
It is even as dark as a winter day.

Henry Atkinson (11)
Carrickfergus Model Primary School, Carrickfergus

No

No is a black word
No is as evil as the Devil
It is as dark as coal
It is as dark as the sky
As fast as lightning
As squelchy as mud
As crafty as a robber
As choking as smoke
As sticky as tar
No is a black word.

Scott Kerr (11)
Carrickfergus Model Primary School, Carrickfergus

Limerick

There was a young fellow from Caster,
Who tried to do everything faster,
He then went to bed
And thought he was dead,
But he just saw a ghost called Casper.

Lynsey Turner (11)
Carrickfergus Model Primary School, Carrickfergus

The Writer Of This Poem

(Based on 'The Writer of this Poem' by Roger McGough)

Is taller than a flag-pole
As keen as a fox
As handsome as can be
As bold as brass
As sharp as a pin
As strong as a boxer
As tricky as a riddle
As smooth as a pebble
As quick as a gun shooting
As clean as a window
As clever as a scientist.

David Campbell (11)
Carrickfergus Model Primary School, Carrickfergus

No

No is like the colour red
No is like an angry teacher
No grows like a thorny weed and sometimes as sweet as a flower
No is as heavy as a brick
No is as welcome as a big black bruise
No is as disgusting as hard lasagne
No is as flat as a homework book
No is as bitter as a grapefruit
No is as hard as the Bible.

Chloe Smyth (11)
Carrickfergus Model Primary School, Carrickfergus

The Writer Of This Poem

(Based on 'The Writer of this Poem' by Roger McGough)

The writer of this poem
Is as cool as ice cream
As mad as a cow
As bright as a sunbeam

The writer of this poem
Is as sweet as a cake
As mad as a cow
As pretty as a snowflake

The writer of this poem
Is as mysterious as the moon
As light as a butterfly
As quick as the coming monsoon

The writer of this poem
Is as kind as a bee
As secretive as a mouse nearby
As true as the writer of this poem is me.

Alex Burnside (11)
Carrickfergus Model Primary School, Carrickfergus

A Mouthful Of Sweets

A bookshelf of flies,
A display board of pictures,
A wardrobe of toys,
A school of students,
A ship of immigrants,
A bottle of water,
A cloakroom of coats,
A school bag of books,
A mouthful of sweets.

Emma Clarke (11)
Carrickfergus Model Primary School, Carrickfergus

No

No is a black word
As bitter as lemon
As soggy as wet bread
As heavy as a brick
As hard as steel
As dark as black
As dirty as drains
As old as churches
As powerful as electricity
As hot as fire
As strong as machinery.

Peter Brown (11)
Carrickfergus Model Primary School, Carrickfergus

No

No is a black word
It's as bitter as lemons
Is hard as iron
Is as heavy as rock
Is as soggy as beans
As welcome as rain
As sour as vinegar
As dull as rain
As hot as fire
As fierce as a lion
As mad as a hatter.

James Simmonds (11)
Carrickfergus Model Primary School, Carrickfergus

My Hamster

My energetic hamster
Loves his ball
He is fast, small and crazy
He is as white as snow
And as quick as lightning
He makes me feel so big
As big as a giant
My energetic hamster
Reminds me to enjoy every part of life
Because you only live once.

Kerry McIlroy (11)
Carrickfergus Model Primary School, Carrickfergus

What Are The Clouds?

The clouds are big candyflosses floating in a blue room.
Clouds are white cotton wool stuck to a piece of cardboard.
Clouds are bunny rabbits' tails.
Clouds are ice cream scoops thrown in the sky.
Clouds are pieces of paper cut into circles and glued to
                                a blue piece of paper.

Victoria Brier (11)
Carrickfergus Model Primary School, Carrickfergus

Winter

Winter, spreads out its arms
Winter, sticks out its legs to trip people
Winter, pokes out its numb feet
Winter, opens up its eyes slowly
Winter wind blows on the winter's hair
Winter opens its mouth to blow cold winds at people.

Aimee Ellis (11)
Carrickfergus Model Primary School, Carrickfergus

Adverb Poem!

Silently the mouse scurried
Swiftly the waitress hurried
Softly the singer sang
Loudly the bell rang
Warily the spy crept

Worriedly the maid wept
All in all the world goes round
Smoothly, slowly without a sound.

Rachel Barkley (11)
Carrickfergus Model Primary School, Carrickfergus

Limericks

There was a young man from Bombay
Who couldn't fit through the doorway
He went on a diet
But couldn't stay by it
So tried liposuction today!

Alex Thompson
Carrickfergus Model Primary School, Carrickfergus

The Massive Football Stadium

The massive football stadium,
Holds up to 69,000 people,
Huge, noisy, crowded,
Like a massive bowl,
Like a massive garden with a high fence round it,
It makes me feel so tiny,
Like a piece of grit,
The massive football stadium,
Reminds me how fun life can be.

Nathan Lyons (11)
Carrickfergus Model Primary School, Carrickfergus

The Writer Of This Poem

(Based on 'The Writer of this Poem' by Roger McGough)

The writer of this poem
Is as smart as Albert Einstein *(not really)*
As small as a mouse
As cunning as a fox

As sharp as an eagle
As sporty as a spark
As talkative as a mouse
As inquisitive as a squirrel

As lucky as a man on the street
As quick as lightning
As stylish as a dog
As clean as a whistle.

Aaron Ellis (11)
Carrickfergus Model Primary School, Carrickfergus

The Writer Of This Poem

(Based on 'The Writer of this Poem' by Roger McGough)

The writer of this poem
Is as loud as a door slamming
As keen as a fox
And as perfect as can be!

As good as gold
As sharp as a knife
As strong as Superman
As happy as can be!

As smooth as a table
As quick as a cheetah
As nice as sweets
As crazy as can be!

Jessica Lyness (11)
Carrickfergus Model Primary School, Carrickfergus

The Writer Of This Poem

(Based on 'The Writer of this Poem' by Roger McGough)

The writer of this poem
Is as mad as a banshee
As cheeky as a monkey
As bad as the Devil

As brave as a knight
As sly as a ghost
As clean as soap
As slippery as oil

As sharp as a knife
As cool as ice
As loud as thunder
As bright as a torch in a pitch-black room

The writer of this poem
Is as fast as a cheetah
He's always good (not)
(Or so the poem says!)

Ashton Corey (10)
Carrickfergus Model Primary School, Carrickfergus

Fear

Fear is a dark shadow lurking,
It's a red fiery dragon,
Fear's an angel from Hell,
It's a claw grabbing your soul,
Fear is a child screaming,
It's a life-threatening situation,
Fear is a dagger stabbing your heart,
It's blood vessels exploding,
Fear is indescribable.

Laura McCurry (11)
Carrickfergus Model Primary School, Carrickfergus

My Uncle

My uncle is very funny,
He is very, very strong,
He used to be a boxer,
He likes to train all day long.

We all call him Bubby,
That's not his real name.
He always calls me names
Like Lazybones and Tall Boy.

Riding my daddy's motorbike,
Racing down the road,
Warm air on his face,
Doing funny skids.

Dale Crudden (9)
Cornagague Primary School, Magheraveely

My Favourite Team

Red home and black away.
Scoring goals galore.
Even when they're winning
They go for more.

Rooney is my hero
Wearing number eight
What a footballer he is
I think he's great.

Ronaldo is my man
He's really smart
He always runs as fast as he can
Passing the ball like an art.

Joe Mulligan (8)
Cornagague Primary School, Magheraveely

Thierry Henry

Thierry Henry
Is the best footballer
You will ever see.
He takes a chance,
That's his skill.

Thierry Henry
Is the best player
In the world.
Curling the ball,
Spinning it into the net.

Thierry Henry
Is quite class.
How he must practice
On the green grass.

Thierry Henry
Is fantastic
Never plays with
A ball made of plastic.

Thierry Henry
He will always score
Goal after goal.
Even then,
He still wants more.

Thierry Henry
Uses a lot of sweat
When he puts the
Ball into the net.

Thierry Henry
Always defending
And sending
The ball to Vieira.

Liam Óg Strain (9)
Cornagague Primary School, Magheraveely

My Pet Dog

My dog Sherrie
Is very, very hairy.
She likes to play fetch
And barks at people
She doesn't know.
Bouncing on our trampoline,
Chasing after the ball,
Jumping up on me,
Licking my nose.
That's my Sherrie
Who's very hairy.
Fighting with other dogs,
Coming home all bloodied.
Pinching food when
No one's looking,
Eating my birthday cake.
That's my Sherrie
Who's very hairy.
Getting all dirty,
She hates the bath,
Shaking her wet coat
Over everybody.
She's my best friend.
She's my Sherrie
And I love her.

Holly Jenkins (8)
Cornagague Primary School, Magheraveely

Puppies

Jumping, leaping, rolling,
Munching up their food,
Leaping in long grass,
That's puppies for you.

Jumping up on people,
Chasing kittens up and down,
Tired but never sleeping,
That's puppies for you.

Ears pricked for strange sounds,
Barking loud, waking all,
Grabbing things, running far,
That's puppies for you.

Walking in the dirty water,
Footprints everywhere,
Jumping up with muddy paws,
That's puppies for you.

On the hills rolling down,
They have lots of fun,
They sometimes bite, they don't fight,
That's puppies for you.

They're soft and cuddly,
They're soft as a teddy,
They're very small,
That's puppies for you.

Cliona Mulligan (8)
Cornagague Primary School, Magheraveely

My Favourite Footballer

Damien Duff has great skill
Running, tackling, scoring.
He never stays still,
Always scoring goals
For county and club,
The blond-haired Dub.
He's the best,
Better than the rest,
When he's on
There is fear.
The goals go in.
Cheer, cheer, cheer.
For his county
He wears green and white.
No 8 on his back,
Oh, what a sight,
For Chelsea it's
Blue and white he wears
As up and down the field
He chases and tears.

Daniel McNally (8)
Cornagague Primary School, Magheraveely

Great Football Names

Henry and Van Nistelrooy
Are great football stars,
Running, tackling and scoring,
They both drive fast cars.

Fast and furious they run,
Both in mad red,
Scoring goals galore
They make it such fun.

Then there's Keane and Vieira,
Two great captains.
Telling the team what to do
Running and dribbling, they are so cool.

Ferdinand and Campbell,
They defend their space,
Watching for those attackers
When, for goal they race.

Reyes and Ronaldo,
Each as good as each other,
Cunning and skilful,
Scoring is never a bother.

Killian Donohoe (10)
Cornagague Primary School, Magheraveely

Football

Soccer is a skilful game,
Throwing, running, kicking,
Passing, pushing and scoring,
No game is ever the same.

Thierry Henry running with the ball,
Dribbling down the grassy pitch,
Passing and kicking to his mates
Until he gets the winning goal.

Roy Keane, such a scene!
Tackling, pushing and nudging,
Scoring a goal,
Everyone screams.

Rio Ferdinand's a back,
Defending the other players.
When the time is right,
Jumping out and tackling.

Rooney is the best player,
Shooting and scoring,
Taking corners, blasting the ball
To the back of the net.

Ronaldo's a forward,
Showing off
When he scores a goal,
Then getting a yellow card.

Domhnall Boyle (9)
Cornagague Primary School, Magheraveely

My Pet Millie

My pet Millie
Is a big boxer dog.
She only likes cats
And is quite silly.
Running and scampering
She bumps into everything.
That's my Millie.
Millie looks like she is
Crying but she is happy.
Millie can cheer you up
When you are sad.
Millie will jump
Like a kitten.
Leap and bound
As high as she can.
She doesn't like
People in overalls.
That's my Millie.
She can run like the wind
I can't keep up.
She will eat anything
Even my shoes!
That's my Millie.
Without a tail.
She can fight like a bull.
Multicoloured, short hair
She has no fear.
I love her
That's my Millie.

Ciara McKenna (8)
Cornagague Primary School, Magheraveely

Mum And Dad

My mum and dad
Are special to me.
They are wonderful
Kind, loving and true.
Buying sweets for me
In the shop.
Buying lots of presents
At Christmas time.
Letting us out on
A nice sunny day.
Going for walks.
Letting us paint
And make things.
Getting a trampoline
For my birthday.
Buying us a pet
From the pet shop.
I love you both.

Lois McCoy (8)
Cornagague Primary School, Magheraveely

My Two Dogs

I have two dogs,
One called Timer,
One called Darky.
They are so much fun.
Lying, sleeping
In the sun.
Jumping up on me
As I try
To put their collars on.
Running after rabbits,
Bounding and leaping about,
Sniffing with their little black snouts.
Kicking the football,
Biting the leather,
Barking madly
As I fish with my rod.
Wakening the fish,
That's Timer and Darky.

Denis Higgins (9)
Cornagague Primary School, Magheraveely

Diamanté

Fire
golden bright
blazing, crackling, glowing
warm, red, cool, frosty.
Red oranges, shiny, frozen,
cracking, slipping freezing
ice.

Jonathan Sloan (9)
Dungannon Primary School, Dungannon

Night-Time Noises

At night when it is sunless
I can't get to sleep
I hear lots of noises
All through the night.

My baby brother rattling in his cot
I pretend it's a robber breaking in
Awwwh . . . I'm terrified.

Then I hear my alarm banging
In my ear
It's like a gunshot piercing through my brain.

I hear someone creeping downstairs,
I think it's a robber,
Trying to steal our valuables.

I wake up and fall out of bed
Awwwh . . . that's sore.
And I realise it was just a dream
It was just a dream.

Jordan Stinson (10)
Dungannon Primary School, Dungannon

What Is The Moon?

The moon is a shining ball on a blackened pitch.
It is a football on a pitch of blackness.
The moon is a silver coin in black water.
It is a flat, shiny rock in a dark pit.
The moon is silver bullet in a long gun.

Graham McKinstry (10)
Dungannon Primary School, Dungannon

Crazy Tennis

Our teacher is always
telling us to do the backhand.

We like to do the
much easier forehand.

I like to hit the ball
Up into the sky

And watch it go
So very, very high.

Across the court
We have to run.

Playing crazy tennis
Is so much fun.

I like to win
Each game I play

But I don't always
Get my own way.

Karen Cardwell (10)
Dungannon Primary School, Dungannon

Drunk

I know a man who is always drunk,
He never washes and smells like a skunk.
He smokes like a train and asks again and again,
'Could you give me the price of a drink
Before I go up the lane?'
I saw him on Tuesday, he said, 'I'm not well.'
I said, 'I thought that I could tell by the smell.'
He said to the doctor, 'Could you cure my ills?'
The doctor said, 'Sorry but for you there's no pills.'
So the next day I saw him he said,
'Son, I'm fine, all I needed was a bottle of wine.'

Nathan Boyd
Dungannon Primary School, Dungannon

A Scary Night

'Get out, get out'
The men shout,
'They're dropping bombs.'

Quickly and quietly we get out of bed.
We follow Mum to the safety of an air raid shelter.

It's cold, it's dark, it's scary in here.
We wait and wait!
We huddle together and feel warmer.

We hear planes zooming,
Then a loud noise.
They have dropped another *bomb!*

Two hours later, we're safe and sound.
It's quiet now.
We fall asleep.

We wake up, were we dreaming?
No, it's morning, it's safe to come out now.
The planes have gone for a while . . .

Rachel Mullan (8)
Dungannon Primary School, Dungannon

Football Crazy

Smack! Two minutes on and I've just got hit in
the face with the ball.
The taste of the blood is lethal as I fall.
I jump up when I hear 'McClung, McClung
get that ball!'
I can smell the fear of the manager, as we
haven't scored at all.
Just then I see us score a goal even though the
goalie is so tall.
Just feel the excitement kill as the whistle
blows the final call.

Jamye McClung
Dungannon Primary School, Dungannon

I Hate School Dinners

I hate school dinners
The beans are like Playdough,
The chips are like soft plastic
And the bacon is like leather
I hate school dinners.

I hate school pudding
The cheesecake tastes like grass,
The jelly tastes like rubber;
And the ice cream tastes like cloth,
I hate school puddings.

The only thing I like are chips in a bag,
The chips taste like lovely chips because they're home-made,
And the chicken nuggets taste superb - just like my gran's;
That is only the only thing I like about school dinners!

Zoe Bartley (10)
Dungannon Primary School, Dungannon

Five Senses

I like the taste of sweets
Fizzing on my tongue.

I like the smell of flowers
Tickling at my nose.

I like the feel of soft hands
Settling on my face.

I like the sound of motorbikes
Zooming in my ears.

I like the look of sports cars
Driving on the motorway.

Stephen Carlisle (9)
Dungannon Primary School, Dungannon

All About The War

The sky was dark and cloudy.
All that I could see were bombs dropping from planes.
Then there it was, a loud explosion.
I was frightened and scared.
All I could hear were soldiers crying for help
And children crying in the streets.

I could see dark green tents in the distance,
Men marching in the street.
Children saying goodbye to their parents,
Looking very sad and unhappy.
This all happened because of Hitler.

Ruth Burns (8)
Dungannon Primary School, Dungannon

My Days In The War

It was a dark, black night.
Germans flying in, dropping bombs and destroying the city.
I saw red, yellow and orange flames in the distance.
I heard bombs dropping,
Marching soldiers walking up to war.
When the siren goes off everyone runs to the shelter.

Vickie Webb (8)
Dungannon Primary School, Dungannon

The Life Of A Brave Soldier

It was a bright, black night
Until some bombs fell and hit the ground.
A solder was hit - he was my friend!
The missiles continued to fire.
No one helped him.
He was left to die.

Joana Neves (9)
Dungannon Primary School, Dungannon

Life In The 1940s

Bang, bang, bang!
Red, yellow, orange
Big, bright sparks in the dark night sky.

'Help, help, help!'
People crying, shouting out.

Zoom, zoom, zoom!
Spitfires flying overhead.

When will it be over?
When will it be quiet?
When will it stop?
Or
Will we all be dead?

Tianna McCormack (8)
Dungannon Primary School, Dungannon

I Am A Soldier

The planes were swooping from the skies.
On the ground I could hear the other soldiers' cries,
My plane was firing out missiles from above.
My ears were ringing from the sounds around me.

I am on the ground running with fear.
I can see buildings on fire and trenches near.
I am wishing for an end to this war now.
No more bombing or shooting please!
Just *peace*.

Axel Steen (8)
Dungannon Primary School, Dungannon

Evacuees

It was a cold night,
The sky was bright like a fireworks display,
My ears were sore with all the bombs,
Sadness was everywhere as I reached the train station.

Emily and my brother Adam, were with me,
Mummy and Daddy were left behind,
Just a small suitcase with some clothes
And a gas mask to come with me,
My toys and teddies stayed behind.

I am sad and scared,
Will Mummy and Daddy be OK?
Will I like where I am going?
Will I be safe?
Will my house still be there when the war is over?
I hope it will.

I'll say a prayer every night
To make sure everything will be alright.

Hannah Jeffers (8)
Dungannon Primary School, Dungannon

Whisper In The Night

A storm ran through the land last night,
That night I could not sleep,
So I lay listening, listening away.
I heard the trees arguing,
The rain dancing down,
The leaves lay down to gossip,
The wind dashing in and out.
That night I couldn't sleep,
I lay listening, listening away.

Andrew Millar (11)
Dungannon Primary School, Dungannon

My Days In The War

Fighting in the war I can see Germans dropping bombs from the sky.
I can see a fire in the distance, red, yellow and orange sparks.
I can see my friends fighting in the war.

I can hear bombs from the German planes in the dark, black sky.
I hear the sound of the air raid siren going off and hear people
running to the air raid shelter shouting, 'Help me!'

I can feel mud on my feet in the shelter.
I feel worried about my children, are they safe?
'When will this war be over?' I ask myself,
as I feel it has been going on forever.

David McFarlane (8)
Dungannon Primary School, Dungannon

Hockey Madness

The very first day of September
Was a day to remember.
When I scored a goal
The goalie kicked the pole.
The other team were sad
Because they played so very bad.
Before we got on the bus
There was a photo taken of us.
That was the day to remember
The very first day of September.

Simon Bartley (11)
Dungannon Primary School, Dungannon

Evacuees

It is a dark, horrible and scary day.
Children saying goodbye, that's all they can say.
I can see the train puffing smoke,
Nobody thought that was a joke.

People running.
Germany not stopping.
No good shopping.

Ration books,
Shopkeepers always look.

Whatever you've got,
Not a lot.

A bomb has just been dropped,
Another man has flopped.

Crying for Mum,
Looking for a new home.

Maybe it will be better.
Maybe safer.

Janine Ferry (8)
Dungannon Primary School, Dungannon

1940s

I can hear people screaming and shouting.
I can see planes overhead.
I am very worried about my friends and family,
Are they alive?
Has a bomb hit my house?
I'm watching the big red, orange and yellow fire
In the middle of the battlefield.
Most of my friends have died.
I feel so lonely and scared.

Hannah Clarke (8)
Dungannon Primary School, Dungannon

The Brave Soldier

The bombs were coming down heavily around the soldier.
All around people were being hit by bombs.
People were crying and shouting in pain.
The soldier had to do something,
He tried to help as many injured people as he could.

Ben Nixon (8)
Dungannon Primary School, Dungannon

My Life In The War

Dear Diary,

It is an unpleasant time here in Belfast,
Dad is away fighting for our country.
Fiery red and yellow flames are blazing in the distance
And I don't know what is happening!
I feel afraid and lonely.
I have been told I may have to go to the countryside next week.
I really wish Dad would come home.

Goodbye,
Love from Abby.

Abby Anderson (8)
Dungannon Primary School, Dungannon

Last Night

I was fighting in the war last night.
There were people being killed.
Bombs were going off!
Sounds in the air were deafening!
People were firing at the Germans in jets.
What a horrible night!

I will never forget last night . . .

Jamie Reid (8)
Dungannon Primary School, Dungannon

The Dangerous Blitz

I can see bombs dropping from German planes.
There are blazing red, yellow and orange flames.
I can hear people screaming and crying for help.
Cannons are firing overhead and guns are shooting.
It is really loud.
Please understand me, I am so, so frightened.

Rebecca Emerson (8)
Dungannon Primary School, Dungannon

Mr Lee

There was an old man called Lee,
Who was chased out of home by a bee.
He came to a bend,
Thought, *is this the end*?
Said, 'No!' and then ran up a tree.

Chlöe Burton (10)
Dungannon Primary School, Dungannon

In The War

What can you see?
I can see big aeroplanes.
I can see crying children.
I can see bloody, injured and screaming soldiers.
I can see cannons getting ready to fire.
I can see guns ready to shoot.
I can see this was a war started by a man called Adolf Hitler.

Darren Gilmore (8)
Dungannon Primary School, Dungannon

Destruction

It was a cold, dark night with huge bolts of lightning.
I found it really, really frightening.
I was off to bomb Hitler's house,
I was trying to sneak up as quiet as a mouse.
I was gliding over the trees in the dark
Then suddenly in front of me there appeared my mark.
I dropped my bomb and left with speed!

Almost at the border, almost at freedom
Then I hear the drill of German planes behind me.
I'm racing for my life through the dark night.
I see the lightning, hear the thunder
What will happen next? I wonder.

Thomas Downing (7)
Dungannon Primary School, Dungannon

Life In The 1940s

I was lying asleep in my bed when a siren went off.
This meant that the German airplanes were coming,
Which might drop bombs over the town.
My family and I grabbed our gas masks and ran down the street
                                    to the air raid shelter.
Here we sat for hours, listening to the German planes, dropping
                                    bombs on our town.
We had to wear our gas masks which smelt awful.
When it got quieter, we came out,
We did not know if our house was still there.
There was a lot of smoke from the buildings that had been bombed.
I arrived home to see if my house was still there.

Amy Willis (8)
Dungannon Primary School, Dungannon

My Days In The War

I can see buildings getting bombed.
I can see soldiers marching through the street.
I can see lights going off in the distance.
I can see boats on the rough sea getting bombed.
I can see soldiers with guns.

I can hear bombs exploding.
I can hear machine guns.
I can hear planes.
I can hear exploding ships.
I can hear armies marching.
I can hear ambulances rushing for the injured soldiers.

Jake Turkington (8)
Dungannon Primary School, Dungannon

Football

On the stands the crowds cheer,
Some hold scarves or pints of beer.
Weather is raining, windy or sunny,
A football match is always funny.

On the pitch the ball is passed,
From player to player, oh what a blast.
The goalie dodges and tries to catch,
The final goal that will win the match.

The crowd goes wild and cheers it on,
But in the blink of an eye it's gone.
To the back of the net and the fans go mad,
What a wonderful match, just me and my dad.

Micah Lambe (11)
Dungannon Primary School, Dungannon

The Unknown

The unknown creeps along,
Finding someone without a thought,
It never warns when it comes,
Just leaving them in darkness,
Full of secrets in the air.

It makes light things,
Dark things,
Turning days
Into nights of darkness,
Full of life now gone
In the empty room.

Kind people,
Still kind,
But lost inside the unknown world,
Walking in the forest,
With nowhere to go.

Unknown is walking up the stairs,
You think there is one more step,
But your foot falls into darkness,
Into the unknown.

But the unknown isn't always alarming,
Unknown is with a loved one,
Walking through the forest,
Wondering what will come next,
Looking up at the stars,
Wondering how did they get like that?

With secrets and wonders,
And pain and sorrow,
Unknown is nothing,
But inside your mind,
Secrets in your mind.

Heather Maguire (11)
Dungannon Primary School, Dungannon

Summer

Summer is like a gentle breeze
The flowers are out and so are the bees
The bunnies run and jump with glee
While daylight comes for us to see.

The birds are singing sweet and loud
The sparrows twitter, oh what a sound!
Morning here has now begun
Everyone's out enjoying the fun.

Janette Trimble (11)
Dungannon Primary School, Dungannon

Christmas

C hildren hang up their stocking.
H ope to get something nice.
R eindeers land on the roof.
I n their beds the children wait.
S anta fills their stockings and eats the cookies and drinks the milk.
T rying to get out unheard, Santa sneaks past the sleeping dog.
M orning comes and all the children wake to presents under the tree.
A nd a dinner is on the way.
S anta brings us happiness, love and joy in his sack.

Leah Cuddy (10)
Dungannon Primary School, Dungannon

Summer

S and between my toes and in my hair
U niform is put away at last
M onths had gone by and I could not wait
M other Nature has brought summer at last
E veryone has fun
R unning and playing on the beach.

Allan McGuffin
Dungannon Primary School, Dungannon

Spring

S un shines so brightly in the blue sky.
P ick the daisies off the green, green grass.
R ing the bells because spring is here.
I n the meadows the poppy grows.
N ear the end people cry.
G oing down behind the hill the sun says goodbye
    but it will come back again.

Jessica Rea (11)
Dungannon Primary School, Dungannon

Sunshine

S is for the sky, way up high
U is for the undergrowth down below
N is for nuts scattered by squirrels
S is for April showers
H is for hundreds having fun
I is for indigo in a rainbow
N is for nice things happening all around
E is for everything.

Aimee Truesdale (11)
Dungannon Primary School, Dungannon

Darkness Of Night

In the darkness of the night,
The moon and stars are shining bright,
On the walls the shadows fall,
Making patterns small and tall,
Silly things make me afraid,
Demons with their swords and blades,
I scream with fright to go away,
But they stay until the light of day.

Dwaine Bradley (11)
Dungannon Primary School, Dungannon

Dreams

I lie awake
And count some sheep
234 . . . 235
Thoughts in my head
Say I won't get to sleep
A giraffe
Has just walked
Into my room!
My teddy bear is
Meditating
'Land ahoy!' bellowed the pirate
And sprung on top of me.
I glanced at my 'feet'
And guess what I saw?
My brother's rubber ducks
'Rubber ducks for feet,'
Said my teddy,
'Well that's a first!'
Everything started to fade
All I saw was black
And then I saw my hands
My normal head and feet
Dreams . . .

Emily Johnson   (10)
Holywood Primary School, Holywood

Night

I like the dark disguise of night.
Car headlights seem like chaotic balls of fire
Flying towards the unfortunates who cross their path
Traffic like meteors from space
Mysterious faces covered by darkness.

Connor Roberts   (10)
Holywood Primary School, Holywood

When The Moon Conquers The Earth

A dark veil binds a bloodstained sky
Trees become twisted, gnarled gargoyles
The screeching owls, their little imps
Steely-eyed moon emerges to take charge of his empire
His soldiers, the stars
In the distant cities, mechanical stars emerge,
Their light guiding various paths throughout the stony labyrinth.
In the following hours the moon awaits
The sun to rise
Bringing dawn in its wake
And once again the moon shall fade
To return and claim the land
Again.

Jordan Watts (10)
Holywood Primary School, Holywood

In The Dark

In the dark no one can hear you scream
As the trees stand in a line

As the wind howls and the trees roar
Something is coming, ooh much more

There are footsteps behind him
Thud! He runs for the cabin
But who else to meet but a man in black

He runs out to see everyone he knows
Turn into zombies

So he ran but they catch him
But then he wakes up
To find zombies outside

He runs for his life
But there is no point running again
They will find him.

Abigail Dornan (10)
Holywood Primary School, Holywood

Autumn

Autumn is . . .
Fireworks exploding in the air

Autumn is . . .
Bonfire flames flickering everywhere

Autumn is . . .
Leaves rustling on the ground

Autumn is . . .
Chill in the air all around

Autumn is . . .
Darkness coming earlier each day

Autumn is . . .
Conkers, fun to find and take away

Autumn is . . .
Trick or treating
Dressing up in the night

Autumn is . . .
My favourite season of all.

Rachael Berry (10)
Holywood Primary School, Holywood

Summer Holidays

Sunny summer days on the beach.
Barbecue outside with friends coming to stay.
Late nights and longer evenings.
Let's eat al fresco, it's the way to go.
Packing away all my winter clothes
And bringing out my summer wardrobe.
Let's go out and have a water fight.
Getting my shorts on and going to the beach.
Here comes summer and I'm ready.
The smell of food wafting from the barbecue.
The one thing I'm hoping for is that the days won't pass too quickly.

Rhianna Uprichard (10)
Holywood Primary School, Holywood

Summer Is Here

Counting the moments,
Until summer comes.
Hey, every child is,
It beats doing sums!

Winter clothes leaving,
We're free at last,
Get in those shorts and T-shirts,
Fast!

Outside eating - al fresco to you,
When night falls, what do we do?
Go to bed? Be bored to death?
I know, let's barbecue!

Sizzling sausages,
In the summer sun,
Friends and family stamp feet,
Perfect summer fun.

Volleyball on the beach,
With friends all having a laugh.
Soft sand between my toes -
With seaweed brushing past.

Silhouetted seahorses, in the sea,
While jellyfish get washed up.
Searching for worm casts in the sand,
While fish get kept in cups.

Summer is a fun season,
I can say no more.
But what I would like in summer,
Is one day more.

Rebecca McLean (10)
Holywood Primary School, Holywood

Night-Time

I love day but hate night
I feel lonely
Look around my room
See the clock but it's still 9pm
Finally think of morning time
Open my curtains when I awake
Don't nod off
I'm trying to make sleep come
I can't wake Mum
She'll shout at me and give me a smack
I wish that morning comes back
Mum goes downstairs, clip-clop, clip-clop
For a drink maybe
She thinks I'm sound asleep
I look at the stars twinkling like fairies
I can't wait to hear the alarm clock beep
To wake up, out of darkness and secret dreams keep
10, 9, 8, 7, 6, 5, 4, 3, 2, 1
Night, night
Zzzzzzzzz.

Shannon Rice (10)
Holywood Primary School, Holywood

Ballerina

Her face is a painting
Her smile is a ray of golden sunshine
Her hands are glass, smooth and delicate
Her arms are graceful swans
Her legs are strong yet fragile
Her fingers are butterflies fluttering in the breeze
Her heart is a lion, full of courage
Her stare is a piercing needle
Her voice is a music box
Her laugh is the song of a bird.

Amy McNally (11)
Holywood Primary School, Holywood

Sudden Spring

Spring has come at last
I have been waiting for a long time for spring to come
I like spring because the daffodils are in bloom.

Kids opening Easter eggs, eating them so quickly
Longer days and nights means more fun
Ice cream of every flavour.

Baby lambs are born in grassy fields
Skipping and jumping and eating grass
No school or homework.

Having water fights and having picnics with my cousins
A nice cold pillow
Cat sleeping on my bed.

Joshua Danby (10)
Holywood Primary School, Holywood

Kathryn

Her face is a scoop of vanilla ice cream
Her smile is a juicy slice of watermelon
Her hand is a soft puppy's paw
Her arms are broomsticks
Her legs are scaffolding of a building
Her fingers are stems of beautiful daffodils
Her heart is full of butterflies, warm and fun
Her stare a sun ray, shining bright
Her voice is a screaming monkey
Her laugh is a squeaking mouse.

Rosie Davies (11)
Holywood Primary School, Holywood

Chelsea Champs!

Chelsea are on the verge of the title.
They have possession with Arjen Robben
Who passes it in for Gudjohnsen,
And Chelsea take the lead.
He acutely knew what he was doing there.
Spectacular finish!
Five minutes until Chelsea are crowned champions
And they have the ball again.
It's Frank Lampard
What a phenomenal goal!
Fans are streaming onto the pitch.
Every player can feel the emotion
They lift the trophy.
What celebrations.
Champions!

Marc Price (10)
Holywood Primary School, Holywood

The Wind Is A . . .

The wind is a howling wolf in the night
breaking windows and causing commotion.

A championship boxer empowered to strike people
off their feet with one swift blow.
Crashing them into walls
and hurling debris at them.

A bulldozer demolishing anything in its path.
A nuclear bomb exploding with rage and fury,
able to bury opponents with rubble.

Wind.

William Burrows (10)
Holywood Primary School, Holywood

The Pianist

Her face has confidence and determination
Her smile is the crescent of the moon
Her hands creep around each octave with sweet sounds
She keeps her arms steady and stiff
Her legs springing to the sweet melody sound
She disturbs the keys with delicate movement
Her heart beats louder than a set of drums
Her eyes bouncing among the magical language
That only musicians can understand
Her voice is a library keeping thoughts inside her.

Katie Watson (11)
Holywood Primary School, Holywood

Sunny Donegal

Horse riding in the sand dunes,
Fishing in the rock pools,
Watching crabs scurry away,
This is Donegal to me.

Playing games with Grandad,
Doing jigsaws with Gran,
Dodging rain with my sister and Mum,
This is Donegal to me.

Cricket, tennis, making sandcastles,
Running away from cows and bulls,
Free wheeling down the drive,
This is Donegal to me.

Siân Walker (10)
Holywood Primary School, Holywood

Rainbow

Blinding glow of light suddenly sails across the sky
Glowing and shining eternally
Colourful pallet of light sparkles and dazzles me,
Masterpiece designed to be proud of!
Dancing and shimmering here and there
Glad to be released from being a rainbow in a bottle
The rain and the sun have united to create a rainbow for you and me
Life when the rainbow slips and slides
A sudden arch of colour draws me closer and closer
Technicolour tones blend into different shades getting brighter and
brighter
Perhaps, somewhere over the rainbow dreams *do* come true?

Laura McDowell (10)
Holywood Primary School, Holywood

Summer

Warm summer days
Long summer nights
I long for the holidays
When school's out
Endless walks await me
I could walk from dawn till dusk
The days pass like lightning
I go from small to tall
Lots of new clothes for me
Watch out beach here I come
I run to the water as I can *splash!*
Ahhh!
Heatwave paradise.

Laura Edgar (10)
Holywood Primary School, Holywood

The Mystery Of Summer

In summer I like to swim in the sea.
Oh but I hate the terrible breeze.
I love going to the zoo
And drinking some Yazoo.
I hate sweaty feet
But I love yummy meat.
And as I go on a swing
I hear the birds sing.
I love going to the park
And hearing the dogs bark.
I see the blazing sun
As the kids run.
They're all playing stick in the mud
And jumping and making a big thud.
The nights are light
And the sun is bright.
Go and get wet
And then feed your pet.
You go up the woods
And you bring some food.
You go and sit
And have a picnic.
You go to Spain
And find it rains.
Then you go back to school
And shout boohoo!

Jessica Cuthbert (10)
Holywood Primary School, Holywood

A Circus Of Fog

Fog
A circus of fog
With free tickets and front row seats
All veiled in silver
It does the most wonderful tricks
First comes the mist
Jumping and twirling like a ballerina
More and more come on
And suddenly it's fog.
The great magician envelopes his clock around us
He pulls it off
And in his place are jugglers
Who pick up the planet like a toy ball
    Up   up   up   up . . .
And   down   down   down
As suddenly as they had come
They're gone
Leaving the world back to normal.

Emily Watts (10)
Holywood Primary School, Holywood

A Good Night's Sleep

The day is gone and the night has come
I jump with joy for a good night's sleep
I wonder what my dream will be
I hope it is about winning the lottery
I wonder what
I just can't wait for a good night's sleep!

Alana Catherwood (10)
Holywood Primary School, Holywood

A Model

Her face is a hundred thousand dollar bill
Her smile, a mirror is polished into perfection
Her fingers are pointy steel nails
Her arms are a fragile china tea set
Her legs are long sticks
Her hands are the Mona Lisa
Her heart is a cold and rigid rock
Her stare is a sharp razor blade
Her voice is a booming echo in the night
Her laugh is a mouse.

Sarah Wigston (11)
Holywood Primary School, Holywood

A Rugby Player

His face is a turtle shell
His smile is a grinning engine
His arms are high mountains
His hands are sandpaper
His legs are long train tracks
His fingers are short sticks
His heart is a ticking clock
His stare is a piercing hawk
His voice is a courageous lion
His laugh is an erupting volcano.

Lucy Rehill (11)
Holywood Primary School, Holywood

Summer Holidays

Counting down the days to come
Until the summer holidays,
Staying up late
Playing on the trampoline
Having barbecues in the fresh air,
Shorts and T-shirts,
Licking lollipops while paddling in the salty sea,
The sweet scent of the flowers in bloom,
Playing rounders in the garden,
Swinging on the swings,
At last summer has arrived.

Rebecca Allen (10)
Holywood Primary School, Holywood

Susie-May

Her face is a drop of golden sunshine
Her smile is a slice of juicy watermelon
Her hands are little spiders
Her arms are thin, delicate sticks
Her legs are bouncy, springy trampolines
Her fingers are birds chattering in the treetops
Her heart is a ball, bouncing up and down
Her stare is a simple, innocent and sweet dawn
Her voice is the Houses of Parliament
Her laugh is a mouse's squeak.

Suzy Harkness (11)
Holywood Primary School, Holywood

Katie Watson - The Irish Dancer

Her face is a shiver to the Earth, full of determination.
Her smile is a warm fleece. It brightens up the day.
Her hands are pebbles, petite and perfectly positioned by her side.
Her arms are splinters pointing south, exquisitely delicate.
Her legs are balls pouncing lightly around the floor.
Her fingers are screws tightly grasping each other
                              in the hope her feet stay accurate.
Her heart is a pounding dog.
Her stare is an eagle, eager for a prize.
Her voice is blaring but not when she dances.
Her laugh is a hyena crying in the night.

Caitlyn Adair (11)
Holywood Primary School, Holywood

My Dad

His face is an egg
His smile is a cool burger
His hands are a dinosaur's feet
His arms are broomsticks
His legs are the size of me
His fingers are very sharp pencils
His heart is pure gold
His stare is a penetrating reflection
His voice is the deafening sea on a windy day
His laugh is a noisy foghorn.

Ross Adair (11)
Holywood Primary School, Holywood

Ellie McKibbin

Her face is a bouncy ball
Her smile is a ray of sunshine
Her hands are delicate china
Her arms are sticks of chalk
Her fingers are twigs
Her heart is a soft cushion
Her stare is a TV
Her voice is wobbly jelly
Her laugh is a hyena.

Rachael Presho (11)
Holywood Primary School, Holywood

Bart Simpson

His face is a deranged rectangle
His smile is two crescents
His hands are two tennis balls
His arms are wooden spoons
His legs are broomsticks
His heart is a cannon
His stare is a demon burning a hole in your head
His voice is the black hole of Calcutta
His laugh is a hyena.

Dean Kane (10)
Holywood Primary School, Holywood

Spring

Spring is beautiful
When the flowers are blowing in the breeze
And all the birds are singing in the trees.
All the animals are coming out to play
With the sun shining bright
Until it is night.

The sheep are jumping and playing
The trees are blossoming and swaying.
What great colours they bring
And that's what I love about spring.

Tom Blair (10)
Holywood Primary School, Holywood

Seasons

Autumn, winter, spring and summer are all different . . .
The colours of autumn red, bronze and yellow
The darkness of winter, those long, cold nights.
The happiness of spring bringing new animals into the world.
Don't forget summer when school is out
Those long, hot days on the beach.
Seasons make us happy
Seasons make us sad
Seasons make us full of joy
They make us glad.

Rose Kerr (10)
Holywood Primary School, Holywood

Silky Summer

Waiting for school to be over,
I can't wait for the sunny spells
It's time to get in the car for the glorious beach.
Let's go in the glistening sea,
Or maybe go for a look in the slimy, slippery rock pools,
By the slimy seaweed.
The barbecue is finally out
The steaming smell of the sizzling sausages,
Eating in the al fresco air.
Then it is time for a go on the shining planes in the blue sky.
Now working in school is over,
Summer is finally here.

Sophie Pollock (10)
Holywood Primary School, Holywood

My Friends

My friends and I always play!
We see each other every day!
My friends are good I would definitely say.
We have sleepovers and stay up late.
All of them are kind and forgiving
And they're always very giving!
We sometimes fall out but we make up again,
We always laugh in our secret den!
We are all the best of friends,
Rebecca, Rachael, Molly and I.

Sarah Frost (10)
Holywood Primary School, Holywood

Here Comes The Summer

Here comes the summer
The warm, hot, golden sun
Sunbathing on the sand
Building castles of sand
Putting away winter clothes
Wearing shorts and T-shirts
Eating delicious barbecues
Licking yummy ice creams
Going on luxury holidays
Now I can't wait until next year!

Chloe Cann (10)
Holywood Primary School, Holywood

Kitty

Soft, silky fur
Black and white
Emerald green eyes
And silent, padding paws.

Stalking her prey
Getting ready for a pounce
Go!
She's off on the chase
And she's swiftly caught a bird.

Other cats laze about on plush satin cushions
But not her
Well that's Kitty for you.

Alex Roberts (10)
Holywood Primary School, Holywood

My Bedroom

My bedroom is my favourite place.
There I imagine all sorts of things like going to space.

My bedroom is my favourite place.
I find all sorts of things.
I pretend I'm a pirate looking for golden rings.

My bedroom is my favourite place.
Mum thinks it is a zoo,
Because of all the mess I make
And this could be true!

My bedroom is my favourite place,
There I sing and dance.
I pretend I'm a pop star holding
Lots of money.
One day I'll go and live somewhere sunny.

Amy Buchanan (10)
Holywood Primary School, Holywood

My Dog

My dog called Rusty gets dirty and dusty.
Her coat is glistening,
She always barks but I'm not listening.
My puppy is idiotic and dumb,
A farm is where she comes from.
She barks quite a lot,
So she needs to be taught.
She is very irritating and is sometimes a pain,
Now her bark is in my brain.

Brett Watts (10)
Holywood Primary School, Holywood

Frosty Night

Breathless, building the biggest snowmen
Mum and Dad join in,
We start a third world war,
We conquer Mum and Dad, 40-0 to us.
When I step inside the heat hits me.

Brooke Burnside (10)
Holywood Primary School, Holywood

The Biggest Football Fan

I'm the biggest football fan,
Even though I'm not a man
I always shout and cheer,
With or without beer.

When it's football season,
I'm always happy for that reason,
I'm not a fan of any other game,
Liverpool is the one and only name.

Rebecca Ferris (10)
Holywood Primary School, Holywood

Night

Filled with different sounds
Creaking
Cheeping birds linger to be given food
Snuggling up in bed
Cosiness
Millions of stars
Glisten down on me.

Michael Robson (10)
Holywood Primary School, Holywood

The Mysterious Lady With Mysterious Pets

The lady who lives next door to me aged about eighty-three
But looks as old as a tree,
She says she has no pets,
But sometimes you see a chimp in her garden
That walks with a limp.
In the night you can sometimes hear
The cry of a small monkey,
Sometimes I see
A big brown thing hanging from a tree
I suspect it's a monkey,
But some people say she has a radioactive monkey
So maybe that's the reason her car never goes very far,
But nobody knows the other animals' fate,
Even though this earns her some fame,
She would not boast,
So if this is not actually true she must have *ghosts!*

Ross Neill (9)
Knockbreda Primary School, Belfast

Snowflakes

Snowflakes flutter through the sky
Making a blanket over the hillside
Prancing and dancing in the air
Settling on top of everyone's hair
Lining the lovely green fir tree
Everyone's in their house but me
It's as perfect as it'll ever be
If you go out you will see . . .
Snowflakes!

Shannon McIntyre (10)
Knockbreda Primary School, Belfast

My Strange Pet

I had a strange pet,
So I took it to the vet
And he said that it had
A terribly bad
Case of the animal disease,
(That by the way
Does not make you sneeze!)
It has a face like a cute little dog,
The legs of a smelly warthog,
Paws like clogs,
Body of a frog,
It has wings like a bat
And a tail like a cat,
Brown eyes like the trunk of a tree,
Pointy ears like an elf, not me!
It is very strange indeed,
But God help me, I love it!

Sarah O'Neill (9)
Knockbreda Primary School, Belfast

Crazy Pet Shop

I know a crazy pet shop
The owner is as mad as a box of spiders
He puts lizards on the dryer.
He puts fish down the loo
Mice in a shoe
He's even got cats in an upturned canoe,
He's got dogs in clogs and bats under mats,
He's even got a monkey in a little pink hat,
But what I want is green as grass,
It's not weird at all
It's a snake, and to tell you the truth,
It's rather, quite small.

Jordan Latimer (9)
Knockbreda Primary School, Belfast

My Crazy Pet Dinosaur

I have a pet that no one has
He is a dinosaur,
A crazy dinosaur!
He is as big as a car.
Every time he sees a cat,
He runs away and shouts,
'I want my mummy!'
He always walks into the door.
Every time we go to the beach
He jumps into the sea
And catches us some fish each.
When he eats chicken
He goes hyper and irons his hands and tail.
I don't know how he got crazy
But I'll tell you this
If you are a stranger to this dinosaur
Don't put your face too near his face
Because you're going to be dino food!

Joel Turkington (9)
Knockbreda Primary School, Belfast

My Unicorn

My unicorn is called Twilight
My unicorn comes out when the stars make the sky bright
She has a coat of silver-white
And her horn glows when it turns midnight.
When I first saw her I jumped with fright
But she's so friendly
And she can jump quite a height.
I love her and she loves me
I love her till eternity.

Hannah Nelson (9)
Knockbreda Primary School, Belfast

Snowy Thoughts

Snow is falling everywhere.
People walking, the sound crunching and bunching.
The children come out to play.
The fluffy snowflakes floating down.
The snow is white as a blanket,
The trees are lined and glossy.
Looking at the snow makes me want to play in it.
We all go out and build a snowman.
You feel like it's Christmas.
The snow stops you feeling awful.
The snow comes back.
You go outside and play a snowball fight.
The snow falls gently.
It gets thinner.
There is a block of snow in the street.
The green grass comes back.
The dogs are playing in the snow.
I love snow.

Aimee Gorman (10)
Knockbreda Primary School, Belfast

Snow

Snow, sleepily snow, soft snow
Snow, crunchy snow, slippery snow
Snowflakes, what a beautiful scene,
Don't you agree?

Snow! What fun!
Making snowmen and angels
Throwing snowballs
And school getting cancelled.

Matthew Deane (10)
Knockbreda Primary School, Belfast

Autumn

Drifting sweetly, falling leaves,
Red, orange, golden-brown,
Crunching leaves, soft leaves,
Falling to the ground.

Birds migrate,
Hedgehogs hibernate,
Hear the bird song,
Going wrong.

Conkers, hard and prickly,
Acorns shine and gleam,
Beech nuts so small and brown,
All this nature to be seen!

Erin Healey (10)
Knockbreda Primary School, Belfast

Snow, Snow, Snow

Down from grey skies our snowflakes fly,
Carefully bedding on treetops high,
Each bare branch has a layer of snow,
More snow misses, to the ground it goes.

Look at the roofs, look at the roads,
Not a spot it has missed the snow does know,
Can you see black? Can you see white?
White is more likely, snow gives you a fright!

Look all round, look over there!
You want to just stand and stare.
There isn't much colour, it's white all over,
Only the trees emerge from their cover.

Christine Collins (10)
Knockbreda Primary School, Belfast

Snow

Birds' beaks have gone cold,
As the snow is falling down.
Fluffy bits of snow,
Are drifting on the town.

People make footprints
And birds search for food.
Some wouldn't find any
And some would!

The children look out of the window
And want to go and play.
They're thankful for thick snow
On this wintry kind of day!

Niamh Weir (10)
Knockbreda Primary School, Belfast

My Pet Fairy

My pet fairy is always happy
She is as bright as the sun
She is very happy to be my fairy
She stays up till midnight
And when it is light
She jumps up and dances.
When I go to school
She cools off by the sea.
She dances around the shops
Buying sparkly tops
But when we get home
She flops!

Ellie Neill (9)
Knockbreda Primary School, Belfast

Remembrance

R emember the people who went to war from
E ngland, Ireland, Wales and Scotland
M aybe to never come back
E ach fighting for freedom
M any soldiers
B egan the war
R ifles at the ready
A ttacking the enemy
N othing stopping them
C rying for victory
E ach one saw the victory.

Michael Anderson (10)
Knockbreda Primary School, Belfast

Snow

Floating, swirling, drifting in the air,
It's just so pretty,
I can't help but stare.

The trees are all white,
They're covered in snow.
It's like a big blanket,
A beautiful show.

The snow drifts down,
It drifts from afar,
It really is perfect,
Like a big shooting star.

It's as crunchy as a leaf,
Yet as soft as the sky.
It's so delicate,
I let out a sigh!

Catriona Porter (10)
Knockbreda Primary School, Belfast

Remembrance

R emember, remember the 11th November when soldiers
  ended the war!
E veryone wears a poppy to remember the soldiers who died
  in the war!
M emories can be happy and some can be sad
  but let's hope they are happy ones!
E mergencies broke out all over 1 million times a day!
M others crying all day thinking of their sons and their husbands!
B abies who have been evacuated away from home!
R eally sad people when they found who was dead
A rmistice Day that's what it's called!
N ever stop or forget to wear your poppy!
'C ause it's a special thing to wear!
E ngland winning the war is the time I like the best.

Amy Kelly (10)
Knockbreda Primary School, Belfast

Remember

R emember the soldiers
E veryone dying
M omentoes are poppies
E nemies fighting back
M emories that fade
B omb and blood with battle
R unning and crying
A nd finally noise,
N oise, the deafening noise
C lattering armies
E veryone dead . . . silence.

Adam Harwood (10)
Knockbreda Primary School, Belfast

My Pet Dog

My favourite pet is a dog.
Every night he sleeps like a log.
His name is Joe, he is white as snow.
He follows me wherever I go.
When he was a pup he was very tiny.
When he's hungry he is very whiny.

Laura McCart (9)
Knockbreda Primary School, Belfast

Snow

The snow is fluttering in the breeze
Falling, prancing with all its glee
It glides, it sways through all the days
But best of all you can play.

The snow is great, the snow is fun
The sun has gone and snow has come
Friends come out to have a run
The snow is great, the snow is *fun!*

Snow floats down from sky to ground
Gently, gently, all around
Snowflakes floating down one by one
Children smile, with all the fun!

Ross Gallagher (10)
Knockbreda Primary School, Belfast

My Dog Connie

My dog Connie is very good,
Every day I give her food.
Connie's fur is as black as night
And when she's annoyed she gives a bite.

Anna Mercer (9)
Knockbreda Primary School, Belfast

Remembrance

R emember the day war ended
E veryone's peace depended
M en, women and boys
E ncountered France for our joys
M any were scarred
B itter memories marred
R emember this forever
A nd always do it together
N ever forget the day
C ourageous had to pay
E veryone must remember the 11th of November!

Catherine Johnston (10)
Knockbreda Primary School, Belfast

Summer

I run out of school every summer,
Finally I'm free
But housework is coming, ah oh.
I wish it was winter
But then I forget
That it's fun in summer,
When I play hide-and-seek.
I fly away, outside my window
Away to Spain,
I count to three hundred,
I get my swimming suit
And go to the sea
And swim away to Australia
And get a banana.
Then I fly back through my window,
Snuggle up in bed,
I'm glad I got a fun summer instead.

Aimee Kennedy (8)
Knockloughrim Primary School, Knockloughrim

Plants

I love roses the colour of an apple
because they're beautiful.

I love daisies the colour of a lemon
because they're beautiful.

I love bluebells the colour of the sky
because they're beautiful.

I love trees the colour of nature
because they're beautiful.

I love runner beans the colour of peas
because they're beautiful.

Claire Rainey (8)
Knockloughrim Primary School, Knockloughrim

Anger

When I'm angry
I go red.
When I'm angry
I'm sent to bed.

When I'm angry
I feel so bad.
When I'm angry
I feel so sad.

When I'm angry
I go crazy.
When I'm angry
I become lazy.

Nicole McLean (9)
Knockloughrim Primary School, Knockloughrim

Sport

I like sport, it's great
I always wanted to ice skate
I like tennis, it's a good sport
But to play it you need a tennis court.

I like rugby, it's very rough
My granny says it's very gruff
I like football, keeps you fit
I recently got a new black kit.

I like swimming in Magherafelt pool
I like the slides, they're really cool
Slippy and slidy, just like a spool
Get out swimming, it's cool.

I support Manchester United
But I don't want Malcolm Glazer to buy it
My favourite player is Wayne Rooney
But when he's angry he acts like a loony.

I also support Rangers
But I don't know any players
So to me they're all strangers
The best team in the Scottish Premiership
That's Rangers.

My favourite local team is Desertmartin
The season finished but in July it's starting
My favourite player is Christopher Bradley
He's the best player in the whole world.

I've never tried to roller skate
If I tried I think it would be great
I like sport, it's the best,
It's better than all the rest.

Samuel Hawe (9)
Knockloughrim Primary School, Knockloughrim

Pets

Pets are big
Pets are small
Pets are great.

Pets are fun
Pets are creatures
But best of all they are loving.

Pets can fly
Pets can swim
Pets can hop.

Pets can sing
Pets can talk
But best of all they are loving.

Rebecca Allen (9)
Knockloughrim Primary School, Knockloughrim

The Writer Of This Poem
(Based on 'The Writer of this Poem' by Roger McGough)

The writer of this poem
Is as small as a raindrop
And hairy as a wolverine
As handsome as his name

As loud as a stampede
And as sharp as a pencil lead
As strong as a crocodile
As tricky as a tail

As smooth as a baby's skin
As quick as a shark
And skilled like a professional footballer
And as smart as a brush

The writer of this poem is brilliant
And in Larne he is one in a billion!

Allen McBride (11)
Larne & Inver Primary School, Larne

Shadow

The boy walks with his shadow
Along the morning street.
The shadow of his body
Is seen beyond his feet.

Like a slave the shadow is,
The boy its master.
So the two have always been
Those many years ago

As far as history tells
And boy and girl walk by,
Over whatever sky.

But what if one fine day
The shadows should remain
After the boy and girl have been forever gone?

Alize McColm (11)
Larne & Inver Primary School, Larne

The Writer Of This Poem

(Based on 'The Writer of this Poem' by Roger McGough)

The writer of this poem
Is as cool as ice
As good as gold

He is as fast as lightning
He is as tall as a tower
As agile as a monkey

He is as smart as a scientist
He is as strong as Hercules
And as rich as the Queen

The writer of this poem
Never ceases to amaze
He's one in a million billion
(Or so the poem says).

Luke Brownlee (11)
Larne & Inver Primary School, Larne

The Writer Of This Poem

(Based on 'The Writer of this Poem' by Roger McGough)

The writer of this poem
Is as tall as a door
As flowing as the River Bann
As handsome as a model.

As bold as the colour red
As sharp and pressed as a new skin
As strong as 7 houses
As dangerous as a flying car.

As smooth as a ski slope
As fast as an Olympic runner
As clean as a surgery
As clever as Einstein.

The writer of this poem
Always tries to shine
He's one in a million billion
(So says he!)

Josh McKay (11)
Larne & Inver Primary School, Larne

The Brain

A brain is a pillow, fat and round.

Cauliflower ready to explode.
Grand, grey rivers.
Like a humungous ball of paper.
A brain is a passing cloud.

A teacher is shouting,
'Put that on a shelf in your brain!'
I can't hold anymore!
Bang!
I'm a puddle of slime.

Victoria Holmes (10)
Larne & Inver Primary School, Larne

The Writer Of This Poem

(Based on 'The Writer of this Poem' by Roger McGough)

The writer of this poem
Is smaller than a kneeling ant
As smart as a solar powered calculator
As handsome as can be

As bold as a big red brick
As strong as iron nails
As quick as a flash of lightning
As smooth as ice cubes

As happy as a soaring lark
As cool as a frozen cucumber
As sharp as any army knife
As clever as ever

The writer of this poem
Will always win awards
He's one in a million billion.

Scott Morris (11)
Larne & Inver Primary School, Larne

No

No is a black colour
No is a dark and mysterious word
No is like a dead tree
No is like a graveyard
No is like a moonless night
No is like a light switch turned off
No is like a haunted forest.

Darryl Roberts (11)
Larne & Inver Primary School, Larne

The Writer Of This Poem

(Based on 'The Writer of this Poem' by Roger McGough)

The writer of this poem
Is tall as a bus
As keen as the south wind
As cute as can be

As bold as a stone
As sharp as a needle
As strong as steel
As tricky as a mouse

As smooth as skin
As quick as a lick
As clean as water
As clever as sin

The writer of this poem
Is sneakier than a mouse
He is one in a million
And don't you agree!

Rhys Maltman (11)
Larne & Inver Primary School, Larne

Anger

Anger is a blazing red-hot fire
Attacking its next victim

Anger is like a big pink cherry
About to burst

It's the sound of a heart
Pumping really fast

It is like a bonfire
Which has just blown up.

Emma Wilson (9)
Larne & Inver Primary School, Larne

A Windy Day

The wind is blowing hard in my face
Hat, scarf, gloves on, I need all the warmth I can get.

Nose running, chattering teeth, shivering knees,
I'm going as white as snow,
It's a windy day!

Icicles coming from my chin
My eyes are starting to water
I can't see through my glasses as they have gone misty.

Nose running, chattering teeth, shivering knees
I'm going as white as snow,
It's a windy day!

Trees blowing, bins rolling, even cars are going slow
As the wind is pulling them back.

Nose running, chattering teeth, shivering knees,
I'm going as white as snow.

Jordan McClelland (11)
Larne & Inver Primary School, Larne

Anger

Anger lives in evil souls.
It is a blazing bonfire like a flaming furnace.
Anger is a shooting gun aiming at a victim.
It is like boiling lava ready to explode.
Anger is a squeezed tomato.
It is like a killing machine crushing crowds to crumbs.
It is a chopping meat cleaver ready to take someone's life.
Anger will tear you apart.
It will try to track you down.

Kevin Arban (11)
Larne & Inver Primary School, Larne

The Writer Of This Poem

(Based on 'The Writer of this Poem' by Roger McGough)

The writer of this poem
Is taller than a lamp post
As keen as can be
As handsome as a kitten

As beautiful as a butterfly
As sharp as a knife
As strong as a weightlifter
As tricky as a joker

As smooth as a baby's bum
As quick as a bolt
As clean as a new car
As clever as a scientist

The writer of this poem
Never fails to excite
She's one in a zillion
(Or so the poem says)!

Kelly Lyness (11)
Larne & Inver Primary School, Larne

The Worm

A worm is a pencil wriggling.
Like a dog's tail bending.
Rubber bands twisting.
Like caterpillars with no legs.
A restless rope.

Moving spaghetti.
A small snake.
Silly string.
A short brown bread stick.

Alice Gault (10)
Larne & Inver Primary School, Larne

Blue

Blue are the waves
Swooping in on the golden sand,
Blue is the sky
Watching over us like a mother or father,
Blue is a Berol pen
Spreading across the page,
Blue is the kingfisher
Fluttering from plant to plant,
Blue is the stream
Flowing swiftly down the mountainside,
Blue are the eyes
Taking in the world around us,
Blue are the tears
Pouring out of a child's eyes,
Blue are the bluebells
Swaying in the summer breeze.

Kathryn Perry (11)
Larne & Inver Primary School, Larne

Wind Song

I hear the wind wailing a sad song
I see the wind tugging at the irritated flag
I feel the wind breathing on my face

I hear the wind blowing cars down the road
I see the wind rustling the trees' leaves
I feel the wind pushing me along

I hear the wind whistling past my ears
I see the wind knocking down dustbins
I feel the wind pulling my hat off.

Jonathan Craig (11)
Larne & Inver Primary School, Larne

Red

As red as a newborn chubby baby's skin,
All smooth and fresh,
As red as a hamster's eyes
After being in the dark,
As red as a Mackintosh apple
Freshly picked from the tree,
As red as a mid autumn tree
Leaves falling every time the wind blows,
As red as a robin's breast
On a winter's day across the snow,
As red as a clown's embarrassed face
After making a mistake in his trick,
As red as a just bloomed rose
At the beginning of spring,
Red as the glowing sun
Dropping behind the summer-green hills.

Aaron Leneghan (11)
Larne & Inver Primary School, Larne

The Writer Of This Poem

(Based on 'The Writer of this Poem' by Roger McGough)

The writer of this poem
Is as cunning as a clever cat
As tough as steel nails
As quick as a flash of lightning
As bold as a brown bear
As strong as the strongest stone
As happy as a flying lark
As cool as a frozen cucumber

The writer of this poem
Will win many awards
He is one in a billion.

Alexander Kerr (11)
Larne & Inver Primary School, Larne

The Writer Of This Poem

(Based on 'The Writer of this Poem' by Roger McGough)

The writer of this poem
Is small as a seed
As clever as a cat
As cool as an ice cube

As strong as a shark
As wise as a teacher
As good as gold
As sharp as a sword

As sly as a fox
As fast as a racing snail
As scary as a vampire bat
As weird as a three-eyed alien

The writer of this poem
Is all of these
And perfect and unique
In every single way.

Samuel Knox (10)
Larne & Inver Primary School, Larne

Boredom

Boredom is a broken TV
It's like a cold fire.

I would rather eat my glasses
It's like all the world is asleep.
All your bones are as good as smashed.

It's like you're as dead as night
Boredom is a deceased sofa, sitting still.

It's someone so fat they can't move
It's like the day when your footy burst
Boredom is as slow as a snail.

Mark Lyons (9)
Larne & Inver Primary School, Larne

My Cousin Hayley

She is a glittering deep blue
She is a hot summer's evening
In a cosy living room on a cold winter's night
She is the sun shining brightly
Casual wear everywhere
A brand new snug armchair
A really funny comedy show
A big fry up, all hot and greasy.

Marie Ferguson (11)
Larne & Inver Primary School, Larne

Anger

Anger is a slimy snake strangling its prey,
It is a barbarian bashing its beasts
Anger is the flaming flight of a fierce dragon
It is the Grim Reaper's grin before you die
Anger is a volcano foaming fiercely.

Sam McWhirter (10)
Larne & Inver Primary School, Larne

Dizziness

Dizziness is when the world
Is upside down and on its side,
A washing machine going to be sick.
Dizziness is like a spinning brain,
Going to fly out of your head.
Dizziness is a pencil
Turning in a sharpener fast.

Jamie-Leigh Wilkin (10)
Larne & Inver Primary School, Larne

Anger

Anger is like a bowl of blood,
The colour of red on your face.

Personally performed open-heart surgery,
You want to smash some china.

Anger is exploding cheeks,
Feeling like you could die.

A big shiny apple blowing up,
A massive fire burning out your soul.

Anger is persecuting you,
It sticks to you like a limpet.

Anger is punching a person's face in,
Now that's what I call anger.

Dean Martin (10)
Larne & Inver Primary School, Larne

Sadness

Sadness is a crate of tears
You never want to open

Your gloomy eyes
Fill with elephant droplets

Then you start to cry
Like a baby toddler

That will whine all day
But stop like a calm ocean settling down.

Thomas McDowell (10)
Larne & Inver Primary School, Larne

The Wheel

What is a wheel?
A wheel is a metal, rubber and plastic sphere,
A car's best friend,
A waterwheel spinning pebbles and mud,
Like a ball of string,
A wheel is a circle of nonsense,
A funny, twirling object.

A wheel is like a stupid energy-producing wind turbine,
A wheel is a circled right angle tester,
A wheel is an 'a' without a curve.

Dean McMurray (9)
Larne & Inver Primary School, Larne

Boredom

Boredom is no sun
And lots of rain.

Like a bird with no tune
A choir with no song.

Boredom is a broken toy
A power cut.

Like a library with no books
The world has no life.

Boredom is a football match
Waiting for your team to score.

Boredom is no sun
And lots of rain.

Bethany McDowell (9)
Larne & Inver Primary School, Larne

Anger

Anger lives on fire,
It's like a stabbing knife.

Anger won't ever let go,
Holding on like a boa constrictor,
Trying to suffocate.

Anger will hunt you down,
Like a leopard in the jungle.

Anger will kill,
Will kill like a deadly scorpion sting.

Andrew Hutton (11)
Larne & Inver Primary School, Larne

Anger

Anger is hair-pulling madness.
A blazing fire, getting hotter by the minute.
Face colour like tomato juice, heat of boiling blood.
Temperature rising to the central core.
Temper, temper, you've been told.
You don't care, you're on a roll.

Robbie Johnston (9)
Larne & Inver Primary School, Larne

Happiness

Happiness is an everlasting sun
A silent play, with no noise
A gentle breeze, like playing lambs
A peaceful sleep, like a baby smiling
A blue sea, like a chirping bird
A calm day, a smooth song
No noise
Happiness is a silent elephant.

Lori Brown (10)
Larne & Inver Primary School, Larne

Calm

Calm is an unturbulent ocean
A sea of fluffy feathers
Like little balls of cotton wool
Merging in the midday sun

The desert of calm
Has simply scrumptious strawberries
That hang from cobalt coloured cacti
Heaving their branches side to side
To master the art of snooze

Calm is an unturbulent ocean
A sea of fluffy feathers
Like little balls of cotton wool
Merging in the midday sun

A cup of calm
Is a lovely phenomenon
A brain of dream substance
Like Dream Topping plopping
Through your skull
Making you want to snuggle,
Snooze then snore.

Elizabeth Brown (10)
Larne & Inver Primary School, Larne

The Waterwheel

The waterwheel is a mixing bowl,
A roller coaster,
Water screams going down,
A liquidiser mushing anything in its path,
It's like a trunk of a tree with no middle,
A waterwheel is a funny machine
Invented in 1783.

Reuben Dooris (10)
Larne & Inver Primary School, Larne

Calm

Calm is a clever, clear, clean mind
ready to go to sleep.
Like a soft, comfortable bed
waiting for you.
Motionless, a blue-green book
of happy memories.
Calm is a pleasurable, thoughtless wisdom
listening to a whispering lake
where no troubles bother you.
Like a patch of brightly coloured flowers.
Calm is a clever, clear, clean mind
ready to go to sleep.

Lauren McCormick (10)
Larne & Inver Primary School, Larne

Anger

What is anger?
Anger is a bubbling volcano
Ready to explode.
Like a raging bull
Charging like a cannonball.
Anger is like a boiling kettle
Flowing overboard.
It is an earthquake erupting
Killing everywhere.
That is anger.

Chloe Wilson (10)
Larne & Inver Primary School, Larne

Anger

Anger is like pulling your hair out,
A train going so fast,
Like a cheetah flying across the field,
Flowing fury, running rage,
Anger is like blowing up,
Pop!

Laura Bonnes (10)
Larne & Inver Primary School, Larne

War And Chaos

We were nearing the end of World War II
Our resources were down,
We did not know what to do.
So all men in our village were registered to fight,
We were scared but tried to be strong with all our might.

The next day I left for war with my father and brother
And waved goodbye to my sister and mother.
Then my sister began to cry,
I knew she thought we would die.
We were but two children and an old man
And this war was just part of some horrid plan,
To lose the weak and save the strong,
We were but pawns in a game and this was wrong.

I saw things at war I will never forget
And when I think about it it makes me fret.
For in limp dead hands I saw pictures of children and wives,
For whom these soldiers had given their lives.
These soldiers died for home and country
And to the length of their sacrifice there was no boundary.

Rebecca Duff (11)
Linn Primary School, Larne

The Viking Voyage

I'm packing my stuff,
It's time to leave.
My brother's in a huff,
A few tricks up my sleeve.

Onto the boat I walk,
I'm nervous more than anyone.
My family, to whom I might never talk,
But I'm hoping now to have some fun.

The boat is rocking,
Side to side.
I'm nearly there,
I can see land.

Finally, I'm on dry land,
Relieved but I might have to fight.
Those monks, they are idiots,
Too easy to kill.

What is this? I find a door.
Opening it.
To my excitement,
Loads of gold.

Grabbing as much as we can,
Running as fast as we can.
Monks lying dead on the floor.
Rowing, rowing, we want more!

Carolyn Humphrys (10)
Linn Primary School, Larne

Disaster Poem

It's been a disaster today
I've hated every hour.
I accidentally ate a lemon
It was bitter and sour.

I missed the school bus
So I had to walk in the rain.
I was terrible at my school work,
And it's driving me insane.

I had to do the washing up,
I've hated this terrible day
It's been so bad,
Maybe tomorrow I'll go to play.

It's been a disaster today
I've hated every hour
I fell into the mud,
And now I need a shower.

Stuart McKay, Christopher Braniff & Jordan Mitchell (11)
Linn Primary School, Larne

Minibeasts

Minibeasts are everywhere,
In the grass, the trees, the air.
Nice and big, or small as ants,
In the garden eating plants.
Beasts can sometimes be of good,
Eating all the weeds for food.
Although they can be pests,
Sneaking in and making nests.
The worst ones are the wasps or bees
Stinging someone, *no, not me!*

Rachel Marks (9)
Linn Primary School, Larne

Minibeasts

Minibeasts, oh minibeasts,
So many different kinds.
I go into the garden to look for them,
They do not seem to mind.

Small ones, big ones, fat ones, thin ones,
Crawling and slithering all around.

The ladybird is very cute,
In her red, fancy suit.
The slugs and snails leave slippery trails,
Along the garden wall.

I wish that I could talk to them
But they say nothing at all!

Judith Cameron (9)
Linn Primary School, Larne

A Butterfly

I'm sitting in the garden
Looking at the sky
When a flash of colour
Slowly flutters by
I pull myself up slowly
To get a better look
It is a lovely butterfly
Just like in my teacher's book
It seems to float through the air
From flower to flower it glides
Red, green, blue and white
Before my very eyes.

Jenna Mulholland (9)
Linn Primary School, Larne

Mr M's Boat

Mr M once had a boat,
What he forgot, it couldn't float.
He said to his wife, 'Let's go for a sail.'
When she saw the boat she began to wail.

While they were sailing it began to sink.
Poor Mr M forgot to think.
Suddenly there was a passing plane.
When it went by they went insane.

They ended up swimming to land.
He was hit on the head with a hand.
Guess who it was? It was his wife!
And they lived happily for the rest of their life.

Jack Eland (11)
Linn Primary School, Larne

Teachers

Sometimes I think, *are they creatures?*
Sometimes I would like to leave the class
But if I do it will be lines for me
Then I will see that I just can't flee.
I will sit in my seat and glee
When the teacher smiles back at me.
Then she will go into her store
I will glee no more
It is work for us.
But then she said, 'You've all worked so hard
It will be games for all of you.'
Sometimes I think *are they creatures?*
Then I think twice, they are just teachers.

Aaron Hall (11)
Linn Primary School, Larne

The BFO

Far away
Across the skies
Over the hills
An ogre lies.

He's 7ft tall
He lives in a barn
He eats cheese on toast
And loves a good yarn!

He's got a pet chicken
That sits on his head
And he sleeps in a tree
Instead of a bed.

Far away
Where nobody goes
Is a 'big friendly ogre'
Who nobody knows.

David Murray (11)
Linn Primary School, Larne

Noises Of Nonsense

I went downstairs in the middle of the night,
After hearing strange noises which gave me a fright.
I heard a squeal in the kitchen
To find it was my dog,
And on the windowpane was a red and green frog.

By this time I was pretty freaked out
So I went straight back to bed,
I woke up in the morning
To find the noises of nonsense in my head.

Luke McKee (11)
Linn Primary School, Larne

Space

Far, far away in the sky
Where no man can see
There lives a little spaceman
Called Jimmy Baggee
He has a little, funny face
Not like yours or mine
And he talks in a funny tone
Does he live alone?
Someday I will visit him
In a spacecraft we will go
I hope that you may join me there
There must be a good view up there.

Jilly Duddy (11)
Linn Primary School, Larne

Whatif . . .

(Inspired by 'Whatif' by Shel Silverstein)

Last night while I lay in bed thinking here
Some whatifs crawled inside my ear
And pranced and partied all night long
And sang their old whatif song.

Whatif I had a car crash?
Whatif I go low in cash?
Whatif I come out in a purple rash?
Whatif I never eat mash?
Whatif I bash into the door?
Whatif I smash a window?
Whatif my parents get divorced?
Whatif I never learn to write?
Whatif I start to smell?
Whatif I start to sing in class?

Everything seems swell and then . . .
The night-time whatifs strike again!

Adam McCauley (11)
Linn Primary School, Larne

Classroom Chaos

9 o'clock the kids are coming in,
Ready for the day to begin.

9.15 and my head's splitting,
Punching, screaming and kicking!

Yes, it's 10.30, now I can relax
Oh no what's this, wet break?
Oh great they're back!

11.15 time for a story,
I don't think they like this one, look Katie's snoring!

12.00 time to eat
Uhoh, food fight, yuk egg sandwiches all over my seat!

Now that they're out to play
I can relax for at least some of the day!

I'm off to sleep for a little while
You see Mr Boyd's giving a lecture about how to smile!

Yes! we're nearing the end of the day,
Here comes the headmaster, he's started screeching
Why oh why did I go into teaching?

Clare McKay (11)
Linn Primary School, Larne

Spiders

Spiders are small and have eight legs
Pretty is a web but not a spider
It's their long, skinny legs that give me the creeps
Dangling over heads from their shiny thread
Each strand delicately made by the beast
Round and round, they work so hard
To build their silken web.

Rebecca Henry (9)
Linn Primary School, Larne

The Monster In My School Bag

The monster in my school bag
Was coloured red and grey,
He lifted all my school books
And carried them away.

I chased him down the corridor
Up and down the stairs,
Through the boys' toilets
Under the concert chairs.

The monster was fat
Also very small,
He was very ugly
His belly was a ball.

I almost caught him
But he ran into a hedge,
I chased him up a wall
But tripped and fell off the ledge.

The next day I caught him
Lifted him by the tail,
Flicked him in the ear
And he started to wail.

The next day in school
He was nowhere to be seen,
I hope he's not dead
That would be really mean.

Dean McMeechan (10)
Linn Primary School, Larne

Travel

I want to go to Paris
I want to go to Rome
Even if people say,
'There's no place like home.'

I want to see London
I want to see Wales
I want to see everywhere
I just hope it doesn't hail.

I would love to go to Sydney
I would love to go to LA
I would love to live in New York
Why don't I go today?

I would love to travel the whole world
And see all the sights
The only problem is getting there
Because I'm scared of heights.

I get seasick if I go on a boat
I hate going on a plane
No matter what the travel is
It is all the same.

I wish that I liked travel
So I can see those nice places
I want to see far away
And see the foreign people's faces.

I want to see what people do
In the USA
I also would love to know
What the French people say.

Heather McKinty (11)
Linn Primary School, Larne

Jim

Jim isn't too smart.
He hates apple tart.
He jumped off a cart
With his friend Bart.

His wife is tall
But Jim is small.
When he was ten
He fell off a wall.

Jim is very strong
He knows what is wrong
And what is right.
He always stays out
Of the building site.

Jim is very kind
He hates the taste of rind.
When you ask him a question
He can never make up his mind.

Matthew Smit (11)
Linn Primary School, Larne

A Hot Day In The Sun

A very hot day in the sun,
My mum said it was time to go home.
I stamped my feet
And there seemed to be nothing there.

Time had gone,
There was nothing there.
All I was doing
Was standing and staring.

I stamped my feet again
And nothing seemed to happen.
I miss Mum and Dad
And all that nagging and yapping.

Caroline Duff (10)
Linn Primary School, Larne

My Very First Raid

My very first raid was just last month,
It was a monastery in Norwich.
When we went in,
I thought 'tis a sin,
To kill them,
But they are so rich.

So one said, 'Hello!' and I said, 'Goodbye!'
I struck him down and made him die.
I felt great,
But then I thought, *wait!*
Is it worth gold for innocent lives?

I started to walk,
I heard someone talk,
I looked, he had a shock,
He froze and looked at his toes,
I killed him there and then.
So that was my very first raid.
Maybe it would be easier to trade?

David Fitzsimons (10)
Linn Primary School, Larne

Uranus University

School started off in a normal way,
Exactly like a normal day.
But as my teacher opened her case,
My table took off into space.

A jet pack came out the back of my chair,
And almost burnt off all my hair.
A spacesuit came out of my table,
But my flight was far from stable.

As I flew up into space,
My table spun all over the place.
But then I crashed into a school,
It was really very cool.

I went into school and heard my name,
Time and time and time again.
Then I got a massive push,
I ended up in a cyber bush.

Robert, Robert then heard another,
Now I'm in trouble with my mother.
Exactly in the normal way,
I fell asleep in school today.

Robert McKinley (11)
Linn Primary School, Larne

Hawaii

I'm packing for Hawaii
Gonna travel there in style,
My time machine will take me there
Through many, many mile.

When I got to Hawaii
I had a great day,
Even though the sun was warm
It was well worth the stay.

Every day was boiling
So I shaded under a tree,
I also had a good view
Of the great, blue sparkling sea.

I was sitting under my tree
Up it was a monkey in bed,
I decided to go to sleep
Until a coconut smashed me on the head.

My time machine is special
It doesn't take you to a different year,
It just takes you to wherever you want
In the world far and near!

Scott McClelland (11)
Linn Primary School, Larne

The Time Machine

I've got a time machine! Where will I go?
Victorian times, no, the Vikings, so . . .
I press the red button and feel a shake
All I see outside's a swirling, blue lake.

Then with a *clunk* I arrive. All goes black.
I open the door and the Vikings attack!
Into the time machine as quick as lightning,
Really, those Vikings are so very frightening!

I decide to go into the future and see
What London's like in the year 2050.
'The cars are all flying! Oh, give me a ride!
The engines are too loud! I must go inside!'

Back in the time machine. Time to go home.
Must press the right button or end up in Rome!
At home my friends ask me,
'How was it? *How?'*
'Well, past and future's OK, I prefer now!'

Kim Hamilton (11)
Linn Primary School, Larne

The Magic Box

(Based on 'Magic Box' by Kit Wright)

I will put in the box . . .
The rev of a motorbike engine,
The bark of a dog,
The squeak of a mouse.

My box is made of
Silver and steel,
With sapphires on the lid.
I will fly on my box to Mars
And play with the Martians.

Ross Mawhinney (8)
Lisnasharragh Primary School, Belfast

The Magic Box

(Based on 'Magic Box' by Kit Wright)

I will put in the box . . .
A fairy's wand,
A cry of a baby,
A twinkling star.

I will put in the box . . .
A laugh of a baby,
Fairy dust and dreams.

I will put in the box . . .
Fairy magic and sandcastles,
And scales of a dragon.

My box is made of diamonds and rainbows.
I will go to a star and dance all night.

Anna Millan (8)
Lisnasharragh Primary School, Belfast

The Magic Box

(Based on 'Magic Box' by Kit Wright)

I will put in the box . . .
A bark of a dog,
A roar of a lion,
And the smell of apple pie in the oven.

I will put in the box . . .
A purr of a cat,
The sound of a motorbike engine,
And the sweetness in strawberries.

My box is made of lightning,
And crystal raindrops.
I will fly on my box to crystal clouds,
And land safely on my chair.

Caleb McCullagh (8)
Lisnasharragh Primary School, Belfast

The Magic Box

(Based on 'Magic Box' by Kit Wright)

I will put in my box . . .
All of the technology in my brain,
Happy memories in my life,
The sparkle of a diamond.

I will put in my box . . .
My first smile,
The purr of a cat,
The roar of a lion.

My box is made of one quarter of fire,
One quarter of diamonds, the colour of the sky,
One quarter of electricity and the last quarter of lava.
The hinge is made of dragons' teeth
And in the corners are poems.
I will surf on my box on the biggest waves to history,
Then land on a tropical island and eat exotic fruit.

Joshua Jared Campbell (8)
Lisnasharragh Primary School, Belfast

The Magic Box

(Based on 'Magic Box' by Kit Wright)

I will put in the box . . .
The first day at school,
A rainbow with wings,
The stroking of a cat.

I will put in the box . . .
The smell of apple pie,
The taste of a frosty winter,
And the scent of a summer day.

My box is made of rubies and diamonds.
I will fly to the moon on my box
And I will stand on the stars.

Katelyn Hamilton (8)
Lisnasharragh Primary School, Belfast

The Magic Box

(Based on 'Magic Box' by Kit Wright)

I will put in the box . . .
A bark of a dog,
A rabbit hard to catch,
My first memory of my first Christmas.

I will put in the box . . .
A smell of an apple pie,
A tweet of a bird,
Joy of people laughing.

My box is made from
Gold and silver.
I will fly on my box
To Santa's workshop
And dance with the little elves.

Laura Rainey (8)
Lisnasharragh Primary School, Belfast

The Magic Box

(Based on 'Magic Box' by Kit Wright)

I will put in my box . . .
The bark of a dog,
The cry of a baby,
The bag of bangers.

I will put in my box . . .
The squeak of a mouse,
The grin of a baby when it is born,
The flap of a bat's wing.

My box is made of ice and steel.
I will fly on my box to Candy Land
And eat till I am full.

Stuart McMillan (8)
Lisnasharragh Primary School, Belfast

The Magic Box

(Based on 'Magic Box' by Kit Wright)

I will put in the box . . .
The memory of my baby brother's first smile,
The memory of my grandad's funniest joke,
A baby's first laugh.

I will put in the box . . .
The first time of Christmas,
The sparkle of a rainbow,
Crystals, diamonds and rubies.

My box is made of real silver and gold.
I will ski on my box to a frozen land
And meet polar bears and stroke them.

Shannon Eyre (8)
Lisnasharragh Primary School, Belfast

The Magic Box

(Based on 'Magic Box' by Kit Wright)

I will put in the magic box . . .
Memories of my dog as a tiny, little pup,
Miss Clement talking about the Egyptians,
The first smile of my second cousin.

I will put in the box . . .
The bark of a dog,
The purr of a kitten,
The joy of Christmas dinner.

My box is made of multicoloured diamonds.
I will fly on my box to Candy Sand Land and
Slide down the rainbow.

Sarah Wilkinson (8)
Lisnasharragh Primary School, Belfast

The Magic Box

(Based on 'Magic Box' by Kit Wright)

I will put in the box . . .
Happy memories of my life,
The scent of a flower fairy,
Laughter at a very funny joke.

I will put in my box . . .
The fluffy feeling of a tickly feather,
The sweet smell of blossom wafting through the air,
The sparkle of a magic rainbow.

My box is made of sunshine and moonlight.
I will ride to the land of fairies and
Have tea with the Fairy Queen!
Then I will sleep on a bed of silk.

Miriam Thompson (8)
Lisnasharragh Primary School, Belfast

The Magic Box

(Based on 'Magic Box' by Kit Wright)

I will put in my box . . .
A toe of a real dragon,
A cry of a banshee,
My memory of an uncle.

I will put in my box . . .
The joy of a new baby brother,
Laughter of my family,
A bark of a dog.

My box is made of teardrops and ice.
I will fly with my box to the galaxies
And I will jump from star to star.

Kirsten Rock (8)
Lisnasharragh Primary School, Belfast

The Magic Box

(Based on 'Magic Box' by Kit Wright)

I will put in my box . . .
The hoot of an owl at night,
The howl of the wind,
The quack of a duck in water.

I will put in my box . . .
A bark of a boxer dog,
The first smile of a baby,
And the grin of a T-rex.

My box is made of gold stars
And silver crystals.
I will fly to the unknown palace
And dance on the stars at night.

Jason McConnell (8)
Lisnasharragh Primary School, Belfast

The Magic Box

(Based on 'Magic Box' by Kit Wright)

I will put in the box . . .
The memory of me as a baby,
At Christmas eating everyone's selection packs,
The roar of a T-rex.

I will put in the box . . .
The squeak of a mouse,
The hoot of an owl,
The grin of a crocodile.

My box is made of diamonds and rubies.
I will fly on my box to the unknown
And dance in the clouds.

Jeffrey Johnston (8)
Lisnasharragh Primary School, Belfast

The Magic Box

(Based on 'Magic Box' by Kit Wright)

I will put in the box . . .
The joy of moving house,
A bark of a dog,
And the quack of a duck in water.

I will put in the box . . .
The first smile of a baby,
A tweet of a bird,
And the smell of apple pie cooking.

My box is made of gold and silver.
I will fly on my box
To the stars at night
And land safely on my bed.

Emma McSorley (8)
Lisnasharragh Primary School, Belfast

The Magic Box

(Based on 'Magic Box' by Kit Wright)

I will put in the box . . .
The purr of a cat,
The magic of a purple ring,
The memory of carousel.

My box is made from stars and ice.
I will fly on my box to the moon
And dance on it.

Anna Spiers (8)
Lisnasharragh Primary School, Belfast

The Magic Box
(Based on 'Magic Box' by Kit Wright)

I will put in the box . . .
Bats' wings flapping,
The roar of a tiger,
The squeak of a mouse
And a coloured block.

My box is made of gold and silver.
I will fly on my box
To the moon and
I will dance on the moonbeams.

Christopher Morrow (8)
Lisnasharragh Primary School, Belfast

Fish

Its golden cover so crunchy and crispy,
Layered with salt and vinegar,
Its heavenly smell wafting in the room,
Just lying there,
Looking so delicious,
Waiting, waiting to be eaten,
Oh, I can't wait,
I take a bite,
Mmmmm,
It slides down my throat
Like a train through a tunnel,
Oh no, it's gone . . .

Samuel Glass (11)
Portglenone Primary School, Portglenone

Snow

Waking up,
Oh, what a lot of snow!
So fluffy and so lovely,
Feathery, frosty,
Cold, bitterly cold!
Snow is fun.
Snow is white and delicate,
But is treacherous
And dangerous to the traveller.

Shawn Wilkinson (11)
Portglenone Primary School, Portglenone

Love

Love is like pink hearts in my eyes,
It tastes like sweet, sugary candyfloss
And smells like a bunch of roses.
It looks like a box of chocolates,
Sounds like people kissing.
It feels like lots of fluffy cushions.

Victoria Wallace (11)
Portglenone Primary School, Portglenone

Anger

Anger is a red ball of fire burning in my heart.
It tastes like toxic water
And smells like a pit of slurry.
It looks like Shrek,
Sounds like a squeaky recorder,
And makes me feel I'm going mad.

Alvin Benton (11)
Portglenone Primary School, Portglenone

Profiteroles

Smooth cream inside the choux pastry,
Defrost, defrost,
Hurry up, defrost!
Defrosted now,
I pour on the chocolate sauce,
Get my spoon,
Get one on
And in it goes.
As the tasty morsel goes down my throat,
I think of having still a whole bowl
Of creamy, succulent, chocolatey
Profiteroles.
Oh I . . . I . . .
Lllooovveee
Profiteroles.

Jonathan McGaughey (10)
Portglenone Primary School, Portglenone

Happiness

Happiness is a vivid, bright yellow
Coming from the sun!
It tastes like a melting ice cream
And smells of fresh paint
On the wall.
It looks like the Earth is smiling,
Sounds like people laughing,
Feels like you can
Have anything in the world.

Geoffrey Moffett (11)
Portglenone Primary School, Portglenone

Messy Mabel's Pocket

In Messy Mabel's pocket,
A melted piece of hail,
A fizzy, whizzy rocket
And a black old fingernail.

Some bits of chocolate money,
A shrill-sounding whistle,
A gulp of runny honey,
A prickly old thistle.

A mouldy, rotten crumb,
A tarnished, ruined lock,
A picture of her chum
And a prehistoric rock.

And what about her mum
When she looks at this mess?
I think she will be dumb
With horror and distress!

Hannah Gillespie (11)
Portglenone Primary School, Portglenone

Snow

Fluffy, white, feathery snow,
Oh, how beautiful it is!
Scenery exquisite,
Trees blanketed in snow to perfection.
No grass, not a sprout of green.
So dazzling, so admirable,
It seems
Like I'm in a fairy tale,
Everything covered in white.
Snow,
How glorious it is!

Amy McKay (11)
Portglenone Primary School, Portglenone

Pavlova

That mouth-watering pavlova sitting right in front of me,
Tantalising me,
It's so unfair.
It's just screaming for me to eat it all up.
Well maybe I should have a little bite.
Mmm, tasty in my mouth,
Its lovely sweetness,
I swallow it,
I feel its goodness going down my throat.
It tastes so good
And it's all mine.

Emma Gordon (11)
Portglenone Primary School, Portglenone

In Messy Mabel's Pocket

In Messy Mabel's pocket,
I found some dirty pennies,
A chewy, tasteless locket,
And a packet full of Rennies.
A little rusted rocket
And a tiny wooden drum,
A broken old socket
And a packet full of plums.
A greyish, rough old stone
And a blue toy car,
A miniature toy phone,
And a runny chocolate bar.

Darren McFetridge (11)
Portglenone Primary School, Portglenone

The Frozen Ocean

The frozen ocean,
Only thawed for two months in the summer.
Icy, cold, wet,
Like a piece of frosted glass.
Like a slippery, shimmering pathway,
It makes me peaceful inside.
Like a falling waterfall,
The frozen ocean
Reminds me of how much we need water.

Lois Forsythe (11)
Portglenone Primary School, Portglenone

Anger

Anger is red,
Just like a deadly fire.
It tastes like tikka sauce,
Smells of burning flesh
And looks just like the Grim Reaper.
It sounds as if bones are being broken.
It makes me feel like murdering someone.

Jordan Armstrong (11)
Portglenone Primary School, Portglenone

Love

Love is a bright pink heart
Thumping hard upon my chest.
It tastes like fluffy candyfloss
And smells like scented roses.
It looks like dancing hearts,
Sounds like lips smacking.
It makes me feel dreamy.

Emma-Louise Arthur (11)
Portglenone Primary School, Portglenone

The Ticking Clock

The ticking clock upon the wall,
Gently chiming in the hall.
Then it reaches ten o'clock,
Chime, chime, goes the clock,
Sounding like a rhythmic band,
Marching out all through the land.
Now it's time to say goodnight,
As the clock chimes bold and bright.

Matthew Peacock (11)
Portglenone Primary School, Portglenone

In Messy Martin's Pocket

In Messy Martin's pocket,
I found a paperclip,
A tiny model rocket
And a mouldy orange pip.

A broken mobile phone
And a piece of crumpled foil,
A hard, white, smoothed stone
And some fresh brown soil.

A soft, old, fluffy sweet,
And a brand new tyre patch,
A little block of peat,
And a smelly burnt-out match.

I would not sit beside him,
Not for a million pounds.
I would not even go near him,
Even if I was legally bound!

Dale Hughes (11)
Portglenone Primary School, Portglenone

A Recipe For A Holiday

Start off by buying new clothes,
Add a pinch of SU camp,
And maybe throw in a good book.
Start to stir.

Melt some chocolate and caramel,
Add a tablespoon of the summer scheme,
Playing on the trampoline,
Whip until it's frothy.

Put in a teaspoon of sleepovers and friends,
A pound of the beach,
A Sunday school trip to the Pitch,
Blend until nice and thick.

Mix in a little bit of family time,
A pinch of the pool,
A glass of an ice-cold smoothie,
And a portion of hot fudge sundae from Maud's,
Then leave to set!

Louise McCallion (11)
Portglenone Primary School, Portglenone

Chocolate Fudge Cake

My mum makes
A big, big, big, fudge cake.
She puts it on the table,
I smell it and run to the table.
I start to examine it
For a big, lovely piece.
I dig my fork into it,
Fabulous!
The fudge melts in my mouth
And runs down my throat.

Stephen Gillespie (10)
Portglenone Primary School, Portglenone

My Sister's Meatloaf

I long for a piece
Of that exquisite loaf,
Its meaty texture I long for,
A delicacy rarely made,
It's torture waiting,
But now I wait no longer,
At last I get some,
Its luscious, mouth-watering taste,
My taste buds tingle,
I long for more,
But there isn't any,
And I only got one piece!

Samantha Kyle (11)
Portglenone Primary School, Portglenone

Snow

'Mum, Mum, Mummy
There is snow!'
It is so soft
And fluffy and light.
It is very dazzling
And is also fun to play in.
It may be soft and lovely,
But snow can be very dangerous
And very, very slippery.
It covers everything
With a white blanket.

Gemma Andrews (11)
Portglenone Primary School, Portglenone

My Friend Teddy

I had a friend named Teddy,
He died, he died.
Mum said he was under my pillow,
She lied, she lied.
Oh why did I leave him outside?
Now that I know he's dead,
I cried, I cried.
I have a new teddy now
And he's got lost too.
Oh, here we go again!

Gerardine McGough (11)
Rostrevor Convent of Mercy Primary School, Rostrevor

A Girl's Best Friend

So many colours, so much to choose,
Into the next shop, lots of shoes.
Open my purse to pay the bill,
Something lovely by the till.
Lovely colour, amazing style,
It's a polka-dotted nail file.

Skirts, tops, trousers too,
Purple, pink, yellow, blue.
Choice of perfume, designer so neat,
Beyoncé Knowles True Star,
Smells sweet.
Get more bags to weigh me down,
And right now I start to frown,
Going home is so sad,
Maybe tomorrow won't be bad.
Wake up early tomorrow morning,
More time for a girl's best
Friend . . .
Shopping.

Tara Morgan (11)
Rostrevor Convent of Mercy Primary School, Rostrevor

Running Race

Runners on, laces tied
I don't want to run and there's nowhere to hide!
I don't want to run, especially in this race
'What happens if I come last? You know I'm not very fast.'
'Don't worry, girls, it's all for the fun!'
'But Miss, do I really have to run?'
The whistle has blown, the race has started
Two minutes later the race is done.
I must say I really I did have fun.
Second to last again!
It's not like I can change gear, ah well
There's always next year!

Ashling Tinnelly (11)
Rostrevor Convent of Mercy Primary School, Rostrevor

Show Jumping

On my horse
Ready to go
Very nervous
Oh no!
I feel so sick
Have to act slick
I love my horse
But this is a new course
Start to jump
In my throat is a lump
Throat so dry
Dying of thirst
Judge calls out
I've got a first!

Loren Rice (11)
Rostrevor Convent of Mercy Primary School, Rostrevor

The Family Reunion

I *l-o-v-e* family 'get-togethers'
They are *so* much fun!
I get to see my cousins and my granny
Who thinks she's a nun!

First Dad gets the garden table out of the shed,
trips over Lucy's pram and *bumps* his head!
Mum floats around with nibblets and cheese
But Aunt Grace never takes any
In case she gets a disease!

We eventually eat, usually it's dark
And the food is that well cooked it tastes like bark!
We play lots of games, too many to list
Grandad might sing songs that no one would know,
Granny always says he sounds like a crow!

But despite the above, I wouldn't miss one.
The family get-togethers. *Yep!* They're endless fun!

Emily Foran (11)
Rostrevor Convent of Mercy Primary School, Rostrevor

Cold Lip

One cold lip
that shivers in the air.
One . . . two . . . three
I'll take you there.

He has hot chocolate
in a flask.
He wears a hat
like a mask.

He wishes it
was a little warmer.
He just wants
a touch of summer.

Aoife Magennis (9)
St Joseph's Primary School, Downpatrick

Wet Feet

Wet feet, drenching cold,
help me, help me, I'm turning to mould.

People say it'll go away, it will,
I'm so cold, I'm sitting still.

I'm freezing, freezing I am,
It's even worse than sticky jam.

I need bed, bed, bed,
Well, that's what my mum said.

Rwanda Shaw (9)
St Joseph's Primary School, Downpatrick

The Inventor's Workshop

In the inventor's workshop
Everywhere you look you see
Materials,
Aluminium, titanium, steel, plastic, rubber,
You name it.
All you can hear is the lightning-powered bell
(it's been ringing since 1978's lightning storm
And it's full of dents).
It smells like
Diesel and sulphuric acid (from when the batteries
Fell into the fire).
His new fuel
Blew up his engine.
That explains a pile of rusty nails
And slates with a black, rusty
Engine.
His safe says, *'Warning: contents highly flammable'.*
Hmm . . . !

Cormac Hyland (11)
St Joseph's Primary School, Newcastle

Under The Sea

Under the ocean in the middle of the sea
All the jellyfish that sting are looking at me
Under the ocean I can see coral
Beautiful shapes looking floral.

I would have lots to do
In the Mediterranean sun
Singing and dancing, having fun
Swimming, laughing, diving deep
Treasures of the ocean pearls I'd keep.

I would be daughter
Of the king of water
In the undersea kingdom, a princess I'd be
Ruling the fish and creatures of the sea.

In the lagoons I'd spend my time
Watching the fish that fly
Watching small colonies of fish pass by
The wrecks of ships I would climb.

And then the most feared fish
Would sniff out his dinner dish
He calls himself a 'great white shark'
His bite is far worse than his bark!

Laura Boden (10)
St Joseph's Primary School, Newcastle

If I Were A Dog

If I were a dog
It would be cool
To chase after cats
And drink out of a pool.

To run as fast as them
I would win every sports day
People think I'd be weird
Even though they would cheer, 'Hooray!'

Michael Fitzpatrick (11)
St Joseph's Primary School, Newcastle

Sick And Tired

Sick and tired, nothing to eat,
Walking all day with sore feet.

Sick and tired, nowhere to go,
Now with a limp, we're walking so slow.

Sick and tired, I can't go on,
First Father's away, now Mother's gone.

Sick and tired, we need to rest,
Peggy's coughing, she has a bad chest.

Sick and tired, I cannot sleep,
Michael is sore, his cuts are deep.

Sick and tired, we walk at first light,
It has been an unmerciful night.

Sick and tired, almost there,
Weak and weary, we're in despair.

Now we're here,
It's getting better,
There's Aunt Lena,
We've finally met her.

Ayeisha King (11)
St Joseph's Primary School, Newcastle

What Is The Sky?

A great blue blanket,
Stretching over the world.

A large ocean,
With little grey and white yachts
Floating across.

A big piece of blue paper in the day,
And at night, a giant has spilled
A pot of ink.

Ben McGrady (10)
St Joseph's Primary School, Newcastle

Me By The Sea

On the beach I take a seat
And finally find a place to sleep.
I smell the water at the rocks.
The sea is waving at me.
But that only happens to me
By the sea.

I sometimes go beside the sea
And jump over small waves
And swim about in the sea
But close to a sandy beach.
But that only happens to me
By the sea.

On the sand-covered beach
I build a sandcastle.
I feel the sand between my feet
Then I lie down.
But that only happens to me
By the sea.

My mum will put on suncream
The fish are watching me
There are some jellyfish
It's nearly time to go.
I'll see you next summer.
It'll be me
By the sea.

Niamh Harbinson (11)
St Joseph's Primary School, Newcastle

Down At The Sea

Everybody down at the sea,
Every child reminds me of me,
So happy and bright,
Not a frown in sight.

Everyone with a tasty dish,
Burgers, hot dogs or maybe fish,
Popcorn, ice cream,
Candyfloss,
Vinegar, salt, ketchup,
HP sauce,
Mmm . . . The lovely taste,
Far too good to waste.

Eimer Simons (11)
St Joseph's Primary School, Newcastle

The Sickness In Ireland

Back years ago there was a sickness in Ireland.
The parents were out working.
The children were on their own.

They had plenty to eat; then they didn't.
They had no cows, pigs or hens to eat.
The sickness spread and Brigid got it.
They buried her 'under the hawthorn tree'.

They were hungry, no food to eat
So they moved on, trying to get some food.
They were going somewhere.
Would they get there?
They prayed.

Conor Devlin (11)
St Joseph's Primary School, Newcastle

When I Leave The Sea

I used to go to the sea every day
But then I had to go away.

I used to play in the sand and sea
From when I was wee, with water all around me.

It tickles your feet, it tickles your toes
And the water sometimes gets up your nose.

I hate getting wet and having to dry
It's so much bother, I have to sigh.

I hate going home, I'd rather stay
But I know I will come back another day.

Nicole McCartan (11)
St Joseph's Primary School, Newcastle

Mary Our Mother

M   other of Jesus
A   ngel appeared
R   ode on donkey to Bethlehem
Y   ou're our mother too

O   ur lady
U   nforgettable person
R   eliable

M   ary
O   verjoyed when Jesus was born
T   alented mother
H   oly
E   ager
R   esponded to God.

Sarah Campbell (9)
St Joseph's Primary School, Newcastle

If I Were A Star

If I were a star I would twinkle and shine
Not in the morning but at night all the time
I would light up the sky like a light in a room
And I would talk to my friend, the old moon

And when morning came, I would say, 'What a night!'
As I would go to sleep making room for the sunlight
And when I woke up beside Mars
I would look down on Earth knowing I was a star.

Aine Anderson (11)
St Joseph's Primary School, Newcastle

If I Were A Wave

If I were a wave
In the Irish Sea,
What fun we could have
Just you and me.

I'd charge at you
Like a prancing horse
You'd try to escape me
And I'd catch you, of course!

With a toss of your head,
You'd give out a shriek,
And that's the end,
I'll see you next week.

Evie Shaw (11)
St Joseph's Primary School, Newcastle

Spellings

Spellings aren't just words that you learn overnight.

They're words that you have to take your time on,
Until you get them right.

You may think you know them off by heart,
You may think you are the best,

But until you know what the actual words mean
You've really failed the test.

Shannon Walker (11)
St Joseph's Primary School, Newcastle

My Dog Ben

My dog Ben is my best friend
He is black and white
And is a pretty sight

When he is happy he wags his tail
And when he is sad
He lies on a bale

He gathers the sheep
And keeps them in a heap
Until I am ready to cut their feet

When he is asleep I sometimes peep
0To see if he is in a deep sleep

He likes meat
And he is so sweet
It keeps him right
And he is so bright

He loves to run and have some fun
Especially when in the sun

He guards my house as quiet as a mouse
Until he thinks there is someone about

My dog Ben is my best friend.

Martin Kelly (9)
St Laurence O'Tooles Primary School, Belleeks

Max

My pet dog is called Max
He is like a rat
He is no height and is very fat
With a coat as white as snow
And a dot of gold
He runs around the house outside
Up and down he goes
Catching butterflies and bees
He likes to catch some in-between meals.

Home from school I come
Homework done, wellies on
His tail will tap the back door
To say he wants some fun
I get his lead to take him for a walk
He walks so fast I have to run.

At night-time I give him his feed
And then he gives me a little sneeze
In his kennel he goes to sleep
He does not snore because he is a dog
If he does anything, it's because
He is my dog.

Annalise McParland (9)
St Laurence O'Tooles Primary School, Belleeks

When I Grow Old

When I grow old the world will be different.
My hair will be grey and my legs will be hairy.

My birthdays will be fancy but without bouncy castles.
My grandchildren will visit me to tell me their news.

I'll still watch football but I probably won't play.
I'll be much too old to kick and catch all day.

So when I grow old I'll look after my family,
And enjoy every meal with my feet up and have a cup of tea.

Callum O'Neill (7)
St Laurence O'Tooles Primary School, Belleeks

When I Grow Old

When I grow old my granddaughter will have to go to the shop for me,
To buy some vegetables for my tea.
On Saturday night I will go to bingo,
I will sit on my lucky chair,
I will win some money there.
My hair might be grey and I might have no teeth,
When I grow old.

Naomi O' Callaghan (7)
St Laurence O'Tooles Primary School, Belleeks

When I Grow Old

When I grow old
I shall be very bold
There is nothing I will fear.

I will visit many places
And see lots of new faces
I will eat very healthy
And hope to be very wealthy.

I will have a lovely pet
And vegetables I will set
Some seeds I will sow
And flowers, they will grow.

Cardigans I will knit
From my sewing kits
Grandchildren, I will have many
And sorrows, I hope I don't have any!

Aine Deighan (8)
St Laurence O'Tooles Primary School, Belleeks

When I Am Old

Now I am eighty I am full of pains
My eyesight is not very good
I wear glasses to help me see
But sometimes I forget where I put them
So now I put them around my neck
I only have a bit of hair that runs from ear to ear.

In the winter my head gets cold
That is why I don't like the snow
In the summer I wear a straw hat
To keep the sun away from my head
Because I am bald
My heart is going strong
So I will be about
For a few more years,
Please God!

Robert McParland (7)
St Laurence O'Tooles Primary School, Belleeks

When I Grow Old

Growing old comes fast.
So many years have passed.
Relaxing my weary bones,
I no longer need to tone.
A wonderful life I have had.
Never have I been sad.
Many places I have been,
So many things I have seen.
As I grow old,
Many stories I have told.

Jason Mackin (8)
St Laurence O'Tooles Primary School, Belleeks

When I Grow Old

When I grow old, weak and thin,
I hope to looked after by my kin.
They will make me my breakfast,
Dinner and tea,
As I sit with my grandchild on my knee.
I will sit and knit and do my best,
Then off to bed to have my rest.

Danielle Murphy (7)
St Laurence O'Tooles Primary School, Belleeks

When I Grow Old

When I grow old
My hair will turn grey
I will have wrinkles in my skin
I will get aches and pains
I won't be able to walk
Because I will be stiff
And need a stick
I will go to the doctor often
And retire to a nursing home
I will wear warm clothes to keep me warm
And eat healthy food
When I *am* really old I will die and go to Heaven.

Maria Murphy (7)
St Laurence O'Tooles Primary School, Belleeks

When I Am Old

When I m old I would like to be
Just like Granny is to me.
I'll drive my car and go to the shop
To buy my grandchildren lollipops.
I'll have my hair all neat and white
When I go out on a Friday night.

Mary Kelly (7)
St Laurence O'Tooles Primary School, Belleeks

My Mummy

My mum tastes like a piece of toast,
Warm and snuggly.
She is like a big teddy bear,
That I can snuggle comfortably.
My mum smells like a bunch of roses,
Smelling sweet and fresh.
My mummy is a kind and loving person.
My mummy is a bright yellow,
Glittering like the sun.
She is a holiday programme - smiley!
She is a woolly jumper,
Comfy and soft.
She is a big sofa,
Cuddly and caring.
She is a rainbow in the sky, colourful.
She is summer,
And she is 'Ards Shopping Centre'.

Emer Gilmore (9)
St Mary's Primary School, Kircubbin

David Beckham

He is a green and white football pitch
he is a football chant
of course he is football
and his building is the theatre of dreams.
David Beckham is a tall, cool bottle of Powerade,
his car is a swift red Ferrari
zooming down the road.
He is a big brass trumpet
making a terrible racket.
He is a bag of golden yellow chips.

David Dougherty (10)
St Mary's Primary School, Kircubbin

My Dad

My dad is a strong purple
A bedtime story for me
A big bouncy tennis match
A cosy cottage in the country
Cups of roasting hot tea
An adventurous jeep that can go anywhere
A harp that plays a sweet little tune
A bowl of hot spaghetti.

This is my dad!

Fionnuala Braniff (10)
St Mary's Primary School, Kircubbin

Noise At My House

At my house there are dogs barking loudly,
kittens spitting at me when I try to pet their furry bodies,
the roar of a tractor's engine,
Ryan shouting and crying,
but at night, when everyone is sleeping,
there is hardly any noise.

Connal Palmer (11)
St Mary's Primary School, Kircubbin

My Dad

He is a mucky, dirty brown,
My dad is a sunny summer,
Daddy is home sweet home,
My dad is a hard wooden table,
He is a funny cartoon,
My dad is a scalding hot dinner
Which keeps me warm.

Dad!

Caolan Taggart (10)
St Mary's Primary School, Kircubbin

Monsters

There is a scary monster under my bed,
There is a tiny one behind my head.
A monster with big, sharp teeth
Is hiding in the bath.
There is also a monster
Which makes me want to laugh.
Monsters are frightening,
Monsters are ugly,
Monsters would make you want to scream
But thank goodness, they are only in my dream!

Jayne Davis (10)
St Mary's Primary School, Kircubbin

My Granda

My granda is a shining yellow,
He is a book called 'The Tinder Box'
And a rough game of hurley.
He's the tallest tower,
A nice drink of fizzy lemonade,
The longest limousine made,
A banging drum.
My granda is a tasty turkey!

Margaret Savage (10)
St Mary's Primary School, Kircubbin

The Colour Green

G   is for the dazzling colour green.
R   is for a hissing rattlesnake slithering along the ground.
E   is for the jealousy-feeling envy.
E   is for the funny-shaped leaf on an evergreen tree.
N   is for the natural-growing grass in spring.

Thomas Ritchie (9)
St Mary's Primary School, Kircubbin

My Mum

I love my mummy! She is the best.
I love her because she is gentle, yet full of zest.
She looks after me like a queen,
Yet she is long and thin like a string bean!
Her voice is soft and my dad's is loud,
It scares me so much I could run outside!
I love my mum and that's not rare,
But what I love most of all is her red, rough, fizzy hair.
                    I love my mum!

Esther Flynn (10)
St Mary's Primary School, Kircubbin

My Mum

My mum is bright red,
She loves Eva Cassidy's songs,
Mum is Kelly Holmes running forever,
And a big tall tower reaching the sky,
Glasses of sparkling shandy,
She's a small and cute fast Ferrari,
My mum is a drum going *bang, bang, bang!*
The biggest bowl of hot chilli curry and rice.

Holly Thompson (10)
St Mary's Primary School, Kircubbin

Granny

Granny is like an orange fire,
She is like a hot spring day,
A warm beach with a gentle breeze.
She is like spring when the lambs are born,
Granny is like a beautiful dress,
She is like a comfortable sofa.
Granny is like a holiday programme
And is like a warm Sunday dinner.

Chloe McGreevy (10)
St Mary's Primary School, Kircubbin

Feelings

Anger is the bad feeling that gets stuck
in the pit of your stomach ready to give out.

Good is the feeling you should have
to feel good about yourself, to run and have fun.

Happiness, the feeling inside, full of life,
care, niceness and love for the world.

Stephen Hiles (10)
St Mary's Primary School, Kircubbin

My Sister

My sister
Is a yellow dazzling sun
On a warm summer's day
At an amazing funfair.
A lovely hot day with a high temperature.
She is
A lovely colourful T-shirt
And a lovely comfortable chair.
She is a hilarious puppet show
And a lovely, cold ice cream cone.

This is my sister!

Lauren Fox (10)
St Mary's Primary School, Kircubbin

My Brother

My brother, he is enormous and tall
Beside him I feel tiny and small
Hiding my toys, he considers good fun
So I throw freezing water on him
When he's in the sun
Some day when I am grown and tall
I won't have to talk to him at all.

Linda Murray (10)
St Mary's Primary School, Kircubbin

Winter

Winter is a whitish sky
With grey and black clouds,
Strong winds and gales
Coming from the west,
Thundering rain which is a pest!
Thunder and lightning flowing through the sky
But I do not know why.
Just because it's winter
Doesn't matter what spoils it
Just jump up in the sky
And say goodbye to the grey wintry skies.

Sarah Quinn (11)
St Mary's Primary School, Kircubbin

The Land Of Make-Believe

There's a land of make-believe
Where the sun is shining nice and bright.
The clouds are made of candyfloss,
The flowers are blooming,
The animals are playing and having a good time.
I breathe in through my nose
And I smell nature,
And a light breeze shivers up my spine
'Cause I'm having a good time
And the sea is made of Coca-Cola.
But then I open my eyes
I am in my warm and cosy bed,
It was all a dream
Oh how I wish it was real!

Tanya Hiles (11)
St Mary's Primary School, Kircubbin

The BFs

Six in total, all great pals
Let's introduce those great gals!

There's tittering Tanya, bubbly and bright
Mice and rats give her a massive fright!

And then there's Becky, far from bashful
Don't blink when she's running or you'll miss an eyeful!

There's hilarious Heather who laughs constantly in my ear
She's small and thin though loves her cream buns and tea!

Then there's Laura, sporty and fun,
She loves sweet butterballs, *yum, yum, yum!*

There's boisterous Bronagh, lanky and tall
Some people think she's in 2nd year
But she says, 'No, not at all!'

Last but not least is wee Eimer Magee
An ultra-smart girl with a fancy for Ron Weasley!

We all are extremely close, mind,
They are loud and proud to be BFs forever!

Cori Marie Smyth (11)
St Mary's Primary School, Kircubbin

A Dog Is A Girl's Best Friend

My dog's name is Molly
She is just as loveable as a dolly.
When she is hungry she begs
And loves to chew plastic pegs.

Molly loves to eat dog meal
But she also loves to eat buttered bread heel
I know dogs are said to be a man's best friend
But in this case a dog is a girl's best friend.

Lucy Miskimmin (11)
St Mary's Primary School, Kircubbin

My Pet

My pet is a dog, a Jack Russell, and she's called Toot!
Toot loves going for walks and I wish she could talk.
She loves me to hit the Camogie ball and one time she ran
into the wall!

She likes to run on the shore and after she always wants to do more.
When we are going home, she never likes to come.
She always has a big drink and something to eat when she comes in,
And then she starts looking like a big fat thing.

When we're eating our dinner, Toot gives me a glimmer
And I know what she is saying, 'Bernadette, please give me
some dinner.'

When we go out to the park, all I hear is Toot's bark.
Toot's a heap of fun and we play together in the sun.
Toot's the best dog I have ever had but sometimes she is bad.

My dog Toot!

Bernadette Clancy (11)
St Mary's Primary School, Kircubbin

Conal

He is a happy green.
The season of spring
Blooming in the sun.
A warm foreign country with a blazing sun.
A bright rainbow high in the sky.
A red T-shirt.
A comfortable leather sofa.
A hurly programme showing clips of Croke Park.
A chocolate cake filled with icing.

Ciaran Hughes (10)
St Mary's Primary School, Kircubbin

My Winter Poem

Winter, winter is so beautiful
Children playing in the snow

Snow, snow everywhere
In the town and in the square
Children playing everywhere

Hail, hail bouncing hard,
On the window and in the yard

Winter, snow and hail,
Put them together
And you get
Winter!

Rebecca Martin (11)
St Mary's Primary School, Kircubbin

My Dad

My dad is tall with brown eyes
and is always sleeping in till late.

He is helpful, fun and great
at playing guitar.

His hair is brown, as dark as the night.
His teeth, so sparkling white.

He'll help me with homework
and will play with me all day.

Nicole Gilmore (10)
St Mary's Primary School, Kircubbin

What You Might Find In A Witch's Pocket

You can find some juicy, slimy eyeballs
and some hairy green frogs.

You can feel her spiky black cat
and her pointy black hat.

You can hear the yells of her broomstick
and the screams of her wand.

Kerry Savage (10)
St Mary's Primary School, Kircubbin

Before The Feis
(Based on 'Before the Hunt' by Lari Williams)

Heavy shoes
help me.
Dancing pumps
lead me.
Celtic dress
show me.
Irish music
hear me.
Dancing teacher
calm me.
Dancing judge
pick me.
Guide
me
through
the
feis.

Brónách McNally (9)
St Patrick's Primary School, Craigavon

The Door

(Based on 'The Door' by Miroslav Holub)

Go and open the door
Maybe outside there's Cinderella getting ready for the ball
Or a fairy godmother turning mice into horses.

Go and open the door
Maybe outside there's a haunted mansion
Or a tiny cottage
Or a queen getting into her coach.

Go and open the door
Maybe outside it's the ugly sisters shouting
Or Little Red Riding Hood picking flowers.

Go and open the door
At least you might see the stars.

Megan O'Neill (9)
St Patrick's Primary School, Craigavon

Tiger

Running in the field
is an orange and black tiger.
It's winning a race.

It's in the long grass,
you would think it would be bright green
but it's not bright green.

It has spiky claws.
They're sinking into the soil,
making marks in it.

Nuala McMahon (9)
St Patrick's Primary School, Craigavon

Before The Visit

(Based on 'Before the Hunt' by Lari Williams)

Long lead
slow me down.
Sharp teeth
protect me.
Heart-melting eyes
Spare me a moment or two.
Wagging tail
whack the enemy.
Loving master
protect me from
the monster in the
white coat.
(I mean the vet!)

Maeve Mulholland (9)
St Patrick's Primary School, Craigavon

The Door

(Based on 'The Door' by Miroslav Holub)

Go and open the door.
Maybe outside there's a fairy godmother
Or Snow White.

Go and open the door.
Maybe outside there is a house
Or a garden.

Go and open the door.
Maybe outside there's a breeze whistling
Or the sun shining.

At least there'll be something!

Zoe McKinstry (9)
St Patrick's Primary School, Craigavon

Open The Door

(Based on 'The Door' by Miroslav Holub)

Go and open the door.
Maybe outside there'll be a princess picking daisies by her castle
Or a magic carpet.

Go and open the door.
Maybe there will be a prince riding on his horse
Going to get Snow White.

Go and open the door
Maybe there'll be Sleeping Beauty, Cinderella
Or Belle dancing.

Go and open the door.
Maybe there'll be a fairy godmother turning a horse
Or a dog into a golden carriage.

At least there'll be something nice to see!

Niamh Haddock (9)
St Patrick's Primary School, Craigavon

What Is Blue?

Blue is the sky,
Light, cloudy and sunny.
Blue is feeling cool
Sometimes blue is a car
Blue is the sea
Cold, chilly, cool
Blue is a task board
Blue is a pen.

But can you imagine living without it?

Chloe McLeish (9)
Star of the Sea Girls' Primary School, Belfast

Smells

I like the smell of newborn babies.
I like the scent of curry chips.
I love the aroma of flowers and perfume,
But I hate the smell of sick and smoke.

Bernadette McMullan (8)
Star of the Sea Girls' Primary School, Belfast

Smells

I like the smell of baby oil.
The scent of shower gel.
I love the aroma of hairspray
And the smell of soap.
But I hate the smell of sick
And dirty nappies.

Terri-Marie Morris (8)
Star of the Sea Girls' Primary School, Belfast

What Is Blue?

Blue is my jumper,
Sweet and woolly.
Blue is feeling cold.
Sometimes blue
Is a cold blue sea.
Blue is the tie
I wear to school
Every morning.
Blue is a pen.
Blue is the sky.

But can you imagine
Living without it?

Courtney Jean Moore (8)
Star of the Sea Girls' Primary School, Belfast

Smells

I like the smell of air freshener.
The scent of fresh air.
I love the aroma of perfume
And the smell of the salty sea.
But I hate the smell of cows
And oil.

Niamh Mowbray (9)
Star of the Sea Girls' Primary School, Belfast

What Is Green?

Green is a chair,
Light and bright.
Green is feeling clean.
Sometimes green is a tray.
Green is a car, clean, fresh, calm.
Green is a book.
Green is a Celtic ball.

But can you imagine living without it?

Catherine Murray (8)
Star of the Sea Girls' Primary School, Belfast

Smells

I like the smell of baby lotion.
The scent of a new baby.
I love the aroma of curry chips
And the smell of bubblebath.
But I hate the smell of sick
And dirty nappies.

Ashley Murray (8)
Star of the Sea Girls' Primary School, Belfast

What Is Blue?

Blue is delightful,
Cold and cool.
Blue is feeling pretty.
Sometimes blue is a sky.
Blue is a jumper,
Clean, calm, fresh.
Blue is a sea.
Blue is a school bag.

But can you imagine living without it?

Katie O'Halloran (8)
Star of the Sea Girls' Primary School, Belfast

What Is Yellow?

Yellow is the sun,
Hot and warm.
Yellow is feeling gorgeous.
Sometimes yellow is a ball.
Yellow is a candle.
Hair, shop sides and a yellow dress.
Yellow is a roll of wallpaper.
Yellow is a comfortable colour.

But can you imagine living without it?

Chelsea O'Hanlon (8)
Star of the Sea Girls' Primary School, Belfast

Smells

I like the smell of flowers.
I like the scent of perfume.
I love the aroma of Chinese food
And a bubble bath.
But I hate the smell of cows
And fries.

Casey O'Shaughnessy (7)
Star of the Sea Girls' Primary School, Belfast

What Is Blue?

Blue is my uniform,
Sweet and cool.
Blue is feeling delighted.
Sometimes blue is a cold, blue sea.
Blue is a sky, bright, free, chilly.
Blue is a beach ball.
Blue is a car.

But can you imagine living without it?

Orla Thompson (8)
Star of the Sea Girls' Primary School, Belfast

Smells

I like the smell of toasted pancakes.
The scent of shower gel.
I love the aroma of a saddle
And the smell of cream.
But I hate the smell of cows
And dead flowers.

Lauren Tumelty (8)
Star of the Sea Girls' Primary School, Belfast

I Can Touch

I can touch soft slippery slugs.
I can touch hard holey cheese.
I can touch squidgy sticky jelly.
I can touch cold runny milk.
I can touch a hard lumpy pear.

Carol Anne Flynn (8)
Star of the Sea Girls' Primary School, Belfast

What Is Green?

Green is a chair,
Hard and bright.
Green is feeling free.
Sometimes green is a hedge of trees.
Green is a 'go' sign.
Calm, clean, fresh.
Green is a ball.
Green is a plant.

But can you imagine living without it?

Chloe Wilson (8)
Star of the Sea Girls' Primary School, Belfast

I Can Taste

I hate the wooden taste of dry cheese.
I hate the smelly old sock taste of cabbage.
I love the taste of stringy, squishy spaghetti hoops.
I love the taste of creamy butter melting on top of hot potatoes.

I hate the juicy taste of pears.

Nicole Stitt (8)
Star of the Sea Girls' Primary School, Belfast

The Taste I Like!

I like the taste of ice cream when it trickles down my throat.
I hate the taste of bitter butter.
I love the taste of home-made cakes that are freshly baked.
I hate the taste of tomatoes that are very sweet.
I adore the delicious taste of sandwiches with ham or cheese.

Megan Joss (8)
Star of the Sea Girls' Primary School, Belfast

I Can Taste

I love the taste of ice cream on a hot day
I hate the beans with a fry-up.
I like the sour taste of sweets as they tickle your mouth.
I like spaghetti Bolognese when you sip it up.
I love hot cocoa on a very cold night.

Alice Doonan (8)
Star of the Sea Girls' Primary School, Belfast

The Rat

A rat eats rubbish,
Rats are afraid of owls and people
Because they are so big.
The rats love the food that people eat.
Rats are brown or black
With long tails and whiskers.
They live in a hole in a wall
Or in some old houses.

Christine Armstrong (9)
Star of the Sea Girls' Primary School, Belfast

Feelings

Happy is a loving feeling. *La, la, la!*
Sad makes a sad problem. *Waaaaaa!*
Angry makes your face red like a fire. *Grrrrrr!*
Shy makes you scared when you see people. *Ohhhhhh!*
Lonely makes you lost in shops. *'Mum, Dad, where are you?'*
Embarrassment makes you see embarrassing people. *Oh my!*
Mad makes you crazy. *Hee hee hee!*
Funny makes you like a clown. *Ha ha ha ha!*
Proud makes you very happy. *Well done!*

Natalie Faulkner (9)
Star of the Sea Girls' Primary School, Belfast

The Library

The library is quiet
No sound to be heard
There are lots of books on the floor
The only sound is the creaking of the door.
Walking along the corridor
How many feet have walked there?
There are old books, new books
And dusty books
You never know.
Sometimes when I'm going there
I wonder where to go.
There is an adults' corner and a kids' corner
There are thick books, middle-sized books
And skinny books.

Beth Neill (9)
Star of the Sea Girls' Primary School, Belfast

Owls

I like owls,
They are so sweet.
When I go to see them,
They know it's me.
Will I feed or will I not?
I think I will,
Do you not?
Owls have deep eyes,
As deep as a hole in the ground.
They have lots of fur,
Like a big furry coat.
Owls have claws,
As big and powerful as sharks' teeth.
I will never touch them,
But I will always love them.

Jeannine Brady (9)
Star of the Sea Girls' Primary School, Belfast

Flowers

Flowers smell nice like perfume
And they are bright colours.
When the wind blows
You hear nice noises.
When I see one, it is so nice
And I just want to kiss and hug it.
It feels so smooth and I just want to bring it home
And take care of it and not let it die
And if it does, I will bury it
And I will cry and cry every day I go to see it
And I will put other flowers there
I might get another favourite flower
But I will still not get over it.

Shannon Bright (9)
Star of the Sea Girls' Primary School, Belfast

How To Bake A Teacher

First you add 9oz of strictness and 5 oz of anger,
6oz knowitallism, then 7oz of shouting,
Some of this and some of that,
Wait one minute, she is still a bat.
We'll need more of that,
We will put her in the oven, *hot, hot, hot!*
Don't put it too high or she will burn the pot!
Ping!
She's ready, put your earplugs in,
She's ready to *shout!*

Shona Campbell (9)
Star of the Sea Girls' Primary School, Belfast

Darkness

His cloak is black
Full of stars
They twinkle in the light
He never comes out at day
He always comes out at night

He is the sky
It's so dark
I'm in my bed
A noise I dread

My curtains are closed
I hear a creak
My closet opens
And out come my porcelain dolls . . .

Mum came in to kiss.
I heard creaks
I saw this thing
I covered my eyes . . .

Tammy Lee Begley (9)
Star of the Sea Girls' Primary School, Belfast

Good Morning

When Hugo and Harry are out and about
They call and wave and even shout
To people they pass along the way
'Hello! Good morning! Lovely day!'
People often call back too,
'Hugo! Harry! How are you?'
Somehow the day goes with more of a swing
When you say, 'Hello,' or 'Good morning!'

Megan Kennedy (9)
Star of the Sea Girls' Primary School, Belfast

Butterflies

I love butterflies so much they make me want to touch.
They all fly in the air like jumping up a stair.
Butterflies fly like hot air balloons in the sky
And when people pass by, they say 'Goodbye.'

Alysha Foster (9)
Star of the Sea Girls' Primary School, Belfast

The Cool Breeze

The cool breeze
Is like a gentle
Hand tickling soft
Skin on a summery
Day. It's like a tree blowing
On me and a breeze gently
Blowing across me and my
Hair blowing in the way. It's
Like a colour of yellow passing
By me in a cloud like trees passing
By me in the sun.

Talona Devlin (9)
Star of the Sea Girls' Primary School, Belfast

Dream Boat

Through the clouds, up in the air
Climb up the stairs, it's a dream boat there.
It carries dreams far away
See the dream land,
Stand up, stand up straight,
You're going to be late,
Going to be late for your dream date.

Shauneen Cusick (9)
Star of the Sea Girls' Primary School, Belfast

How To Make A Friend

First work out how to be kind.
Then look out for someone
You would like to be friends with.
Sit down beside them, talk to them.
Say something nice about them.
Ask them to play with you.
And that's how you make a friend,
A best friend.

Caoimhe Diamond (9)
Star of the Sea Girls' Primary School, Belfast

The Soft Breeze Blows

The soft breeze blows past the houses
As if to knock them down
But it doesn't, it passes in and out of them
And goes all around.
If you were to stand on a chimney top
You would not hear a sound
But you can still feel the soft ballet dancers
Falling off the leaves.
You cannot see it, only in the movement
Of the swishing trees.

Sarah Louise Harper (9)
Star of the Sea Girls' Primary School, Belfast

Ice Cream

Ice cream is cold. Ice cream is sweet.
You can't eat ice cream in the winter because it will freeze you.
Everyone can get ice cream and they always seem to like it.
You can eat ice cream in the summer.
I like ice cream because it cools you down.

Nicole Brown (8)
Star of the Sea Girls' Primary School, Belfast

Sheep

Leap through the field
Like little fluffy clouds
That give us wool
To go to school
And keep us nice and warm,
   Sheep.

Emily Bell (9)
The Cope Primary School, Armagh

About A Rabbit

I found a rabbit in my garden
He sat there all day long
He stared at me and twitched his nose
While I sang a happy song!

Sarah-Louise Halligan (10)
The Cope Primary School, Armagh

Birds

Swift and gliding,
Across the sky,
Brown, white and black,
Watch them fly.

Over the treetop,
Over the grass,
Birds, I tell you,
Are as bold as brass.

Laura Brown (10)
The Cope Primary School, Armagh

My Shoes

My shoes are too small for me,
But I don't care.
My mum is always complaining.
My dad is always shouting.

But I don't care!

My shoes have holes in them.
My shoes smell, I wonder why!
My shoes are girly.

But I don't care!

Everyone laughs at me.
Everyone stares at me,
And Mum always says,
'You're fine apart from the shoes.'

But I don't care!

Dora Nesbitt (10)
The Cope Primary School, Armagh

Lions

Lions are furious,
Naughty and serious,
If you see one, run,
Or you might be too late.
But the lion might be
Happy and kind and generous
And maybe he'll help you!

Michael Hook (9)
The Cope Primary School, Armagh

Smile

I smile when I'm happy
I smile when I'm glad

I smile when I'm laughing
But not when I'm sad.

Jade Coleman (10)
The Cope Primary School, Armagh

What The Cat Brought In

On Monday the cat brought an ugly bird that was dead.
On Tuesday it had a smelly rat's head.
On Wednesday it had an old dead frog.
On Thursday it brought in a fluffy dog.
On Friday it had a smelly old lamb.
On Saturday it had a prickly porcupine.
On Sunday it got hit by a car.
We had a funeral in the bar!

Gareth Paisley (8)
Toreagh Primary School, Larne

What The Cat Brought In

On Monday the cat brought in a bird's house.
On Tuesday the cat brought in a crafty mouse.
On Wednesday the cat brought in Tony Blair's hat.
On Thursday the cat brought in his own mat.
On Friday the cat brought in a bee.
On Saturday the cat brought in me!
On Sunday the cat brought me to the bin,
And he looked at me with a silly grin!

Marc Robinson (8)
Toreagh Primary School, Larne

What Happened On Holiday

On Monday we were rushing down to the plane.
On Tuesday we landed and saw a hurricane.
On Wednesday we went to a fun water park.
On Thursday we went and walked in the dark.
On Friday we went to see our new holiday home.
On Saturday my friend called me on the phone.
On Sunday there was thunder and lightning.
A tree fell down, it was so frightening!

Keeleigh Hamilton (8)
Toreagh Primary School, Larne

What I Dreamt

On Monday night I dreamt I had a gigantic fright.
On Tuesday I sat up all night.
On Wednesday I dreamt of hitting.
On Thursday I dreamt of simply sitting.
On Friday I dreamt of having a rat.
On Saturday I dreamt of wearing a clown's hat.
On Sunday I dreamt of learning to fly,
And when I did, I began to cry!

Stuart Andrews (8)
Toreagh Primary School, Larne

Old Man Din Din

On Monday Old Man Din Din made some porridge.
On Tuesday Old Man Din Din ate an orange.
On Wednesday Old Man Din Din made a pie.
On Thursday Old Man Din Din ate a fry.
On Friday Old Man Din Din ate a carrot.
On Saturday Old Man Din Din ate a whole parrot.
On Sunday Old Man Din Din ate a snail
And with it he ate a piece of blue whale.

Josh Hunter (8)
Toreagh Primary School, Larne

Our Great Holiday!

On Monday we got on a Flyby plane.
On Tuesday it started to drizzle with rain.
On Wednesday we went around Inverness town.
On Thursday we spent one hundred pounds!
On Friday we went to an amusement park.
On Saturday we saw our good friend Mark.
On Sunday we sat 'til the end of the day,
We were glad to get away.

Andrew Weatherup (9)
Toreagh Primary School, Larne

What I Dreamt

On Monday I dreamt of a Barbie doll.
On Tuesday I dreamt of the cat up the wall.
On Wednesday I dreamt of a dead rat.
On Thursday I dreamt of a very bad bat.
On Friday I dreamt of a dancing bear.
On Saturday I dreamt I was covered in hair.
On Sunday I dreamt of a dog biting me,
Then he went to the door and took away the key!

Kirbi Stewart (9)
Toreagh Primary School, Larne

What The Kitty Cat Did

On Monday the cat gave me a scratch.
On Tuesday the scratch turned into a rash.
On Wednesday the cat brought in millions of stones.
On Thursday he gave a colossal moan.
On Friday the cat brought in dead animal skins.
On Saturday he dragged in a rusty bin.
On Sunday the cat brought in a dead rat,
He jumped on the rat and the rat went *splat!*

Jonathon Barry (8)
Toreagh Primary School, Larne

What I Dreamt

On Monday night I dreamt I had a fight.
On Tuesday night I sat up all night.
On Wednesday I dreamt of a massive monster pie.
On Thursday I dreamt I learnt to fly.
On Friday I dreamt of playing monster football.
On Saturday I dreamt I made myself small.
On Sunday I had the best dream,
I dreamt I ate loads of ice cream.

Philip Buchanan (8)
Toreagh Primary School, Larne

What The Cat Brought In

On Monday the cat got a scruffy fox's tail.
On Tuesday it chewed on a sharp rabbit nail
On Wednesday it got a horrible frog.
On Thursday it caught a prickly hog.
On Friday it brought in a dribbling mouse.
On Saturday it carried in the poor mouse's house.
On Sunday because it ate all the horrible things
It was sick and it never brought in anything!

Sophie McDonald (8)
Toreagh Primary School, Larne

My Cat

On Monday the cat brought a purple rat.
On Tuesday the cat sat on the rugged mat.
On Wednesday the cat thought he was fat.
On Thursday the cat found a disgusting hat.
On Friday the cat had a nap on a bat.
On Saturday the cat had to pay the VAT.
On Sunday the cat jumped on my lap.
So I gave it a well-needed pat!

Michael Wilson (9)
Toreagh Primary School, Larne

The Horrific Holiday

On Monday we flew over Belfast Lough.
On Tuesday we travelled on a ghost train,
Now that was a shock!
On Wednesday we played in a pretend sword fight.
On Thursday James lifted a weight with all his might,
On Friday we had a well-earned rest,
On Saturday Mum bought me a souvenir vest,
On Sunday I was very sick
And every day Mum had to rub on 'Vick'.

Joshua Clarke (9)
Toreagh Primary School, Larne

What I Dreamt

On Monday I dreamt I was an army man.
On Tuesday I dreamt that schools were banned.
On Wednesday I dreamt I lived on a farm.
On Thursday I dreamt that my bull did my farm great harm.
On Friday I dreamt I was in World War II.
On Saturday I dreamt Hitler drowned in the loo.
On Sunday I dreamt I ran out of petrol,
I was so angry I couldn't drive my Vectra.

Conor Brines (9)
Toreagh Primary School, Larne

Mum's Dinners

On Monday we had a plate of steaming potatoes.
On Tuesday we had some squishy tomatoes.
On Wednesday we had hard spuds.
On Thursday we had chicken that tasted like soapsuds.
On Friday we had a pile of beautiful spaghetti.
On Saturday Dad had nothing ready!
On Sunday all we had were leftovers,
We were glad when it was over.

Hannah McBride (8)
Toreagh Primary School, Larne

Disgusting Dinners

On Monday we had slimy stew.
On Tuesday we had sandwiches with a horrible hue.
On Wednesday we had steak and mouldy spuds.
On Thursday we had custard that looked like the cow's cud.
On Friday we had curried vegetables and gooey rice.
On Saturday we had roasted lice.
On Sunday we had raw pig and goose,
Fortunately for us, the goose went loose!

Thomas Magee (9)
Toreagh Primary School, Larne

What I Dreamt

On Monday I dreamt of T-rex in the house.
I Tuesday I dreamt of a head of a mouse.
On Wednesday I dreamt I jumped off a plane.
On Thursday I dreamt I did it again.
On Friday I dreamt I forgot the parachute.
On Saturday I dreamt I shot my own boot.
On Sunday I dreamt I bought a ticket to France,
And on the plane I did a little dance.

Edward Horner (9)
Toreagh Primary School, Larne

Mum's Dinners

On Monday we had fish, yuck!
On Tuesday we ate more muck!
On Wednesday we had mashed spuds.
On Thursday we had tomato soapsuds.
On Friday we ate cold porridge.
On Saturday we ate peas from storage.
On Sunday we had hard stew,
The stew was so hard I couldn't poo!

Carrie-Leigh Saunderson (9)
Toreagh Primary School, Larne

My Mate

A swimming lover,
A technology kid,
A 'let's-try-something-new' liker,
A generous sharer,
A sporty girl,
A forgiving friend,
An animal carer,
A jewellery wearer,
An independent worker,
An ungirly girl.

Zoë Buchanan (11)
Toreagh Primary School, Larne

My Mate

A helpful heart,
An honest person,
A kind giver,
A trustworthy mind,
A sharing personality,
A hilarious soul,
A pleasant talker,
A good listener,
A well-mannered partner,
A forgiving friend.

Andrew Barry (9)
Toreagh Primary School, Larne

My Mate

A keen sports player,
An extremely friendly person,
A humorous friend,
An independent partner,
A very outgoing person,
A school disliker,
A PS2 adorer,
A junk food lover,
A polite child,
A good-natured kid.

Jonathan Holmes (11)
Toreagh Primary School, Larne

My Mate

A forgiving lover,
A sharing friend,
A well-mannered eater,
A thoughtful soother,
A creature story-teller,
An honourable boy,
A careful talker,
A sporty person,
A good truster,
A helpful enjoyer.

John McKeen (10)
Toreagh Primary School, Larne

What Happened On Holiday

On Monday we went to the local beach.
On Tuesday we listened to the President's speech.
On Wednesday we swam in the wavy pool.
On Thursday Mum made us dress up real cool.
On Friday we phoned Gran.
On Saturday Dad hired a van.
On Sunday it was time to go home and we left our holiday
all alone.

Kerrie Anderson (8)
Toreagh Primary School, Larne

My Mate

A friendly comfort,
An understanding listener,
A considerate friend,
An animal lover,
A caring forgiver,
An interesting talker,
A sweet maniac,
An athletic friend,
A polite talker and
A trustworthy secret-keeper.

Heather Anderson (11)
Toreagh Primary School, Larne